Southern Living® Cookbook Library

The Creole Cookbook

Library of Congress Catalog Number: 76–41574
ISBN: 0–8487–0331–6

Cover: Glazed Ribs of Pork (page 55)
Left: Exciting Lamb Casserole (page 60)

contents

Avocado Omelet (page 130)

preface

Of all the diverse ways of preparing foods Americans have, none is quite so honored or praised as Creole cookery. Originating with a combination of French, Spanish, African, and Indian methods and foods, Creole cuisine is an adventure in cooking and eating palate-tingling dishes.

Some of the jealously guarded Creole recipes are handed down from one generation to another of the few remaining Creole families or they are the prized possessions of great New Orleans restaurants. But many other Creole recipes have been enjoyed for years in southern families throughout the Southland. The women from these families generously shared their treasured recipes with us. It is from these recipes that we prepared this Southern Living *Creole Cookbook.*

In these pages you'll discover how to prepare Creole-style soups and gumbos . . . salads . . . meats . . . fowl and game . . . seafood . . . vegetables . . . egg, cheese, and cereal dishes . . . desserts and beverages . . . sauces and accompaniments . . . and breads. You'll discover all the tricks of slow cooking, seasoning, and food combinations that go into making Creole cooking the adventure it is.

For all of you who have ever wanted weeks and weeks to explore the restaurants and cooking of New Orleans, this is your cookbook. From our kitchens to yours, welcome to the wonderful world of cooking — Creole style!

For over two hundred years, the Creole people of New Orleans and its surrounding countryside have remained a mystery to their fellow Southerners and to Americans in general. People admire their architecture, their superb gardens, their lovely city, and most especially, their inimitable cuisine. But few people know who or what the Creoles are. And without this knowledge, an appreciation of the highly flavored, savory foods that make up Creole cookery is impossible.

Dominating Creole life, thought, and activities is a lifestyle. It is compounded in part of the manners that prevailed in the eighteenth century French court from which many of the Creole's ancestors came. Overlying this foundation is the elegance of feudal Spanish lords who were also fore-

FUNDAMENTALS OF

creole cookery

bears of the Creole people. This lifestyle is characterized by distinctive work patterns, leisure activities, habits of speech, and ways of preparing foods. In short, the Creole lifestyle combines the volatility and excitement of the French and Spanish with a slow pace of life enforced by the hot and humid climate typical of southern Louisiana and the Mississippi Delta.

Yet with all his love for life and for its excitement, there is a certain sense of economy in the Creole — a heritage in part from his French forebears and in part from a history of living off the land for generations. These diverse elements — elegance and economy — are perhaps nowhere else so apparent as they are in the rich and varied Creole cuisine.

THE FRENCH

The Creole cuisine, like the Creole people, has its beginnings in the late eighteenth century after the French explorer LaSalle returned to France with enthusiastic reports about the New World he had claimed for France. This world, LaSalle reported, extended from the Gulf of St. Lawrence in northern Canada halfway across the North American continent and followed the course of the Mississippi River to the rich deposits at its mouth. His reports encouraged many daring explorers to settle in New France. Two such adventurers were the LeMoyne brothers. With the help of their patron, the Duc d'Orleans (brother of the King), these two men explored a vast area ranging from New Orleans on the west to present-day Pensacola on the east. The brothers, Pierre, Sieur d'Iberville, and Jean Baptiste, Sieur de Bienville, encouraged emigrants to leave France and begin a thriving community in these regions. Under their aegis, there were 27 French families living in Louisiana by 1717.

Unlike many of the New World immigrants, these French families were comprised of men and women accustomed to power and property. They were members of the upper classes, whose emigration was actively encouraged by the king. Their purpose in settling coastal Louisiana was twofold: they sought to increase their own wealth while extending the power — and the lifestyle — of the French court. Accustomed to thinking of themselves as above ordinary people and to associating only with their own class, these French settlers brought with them the seeds of an isolationism that was to be of critical importance in the later development of all things Creole, particularly its cuisine.

The economy of French Louisiana was predominantly agricultural. And the rich alluvial deposits at the mouth of the Mississippi ensured fertile soil for a broad range of crops. It was inevitable that large land holdings would be transformed into self-sustaining plantations whose owners, following the traditions of their French forebears, became absentee landlords. The enormous profits of such plantations were used to build the exquisite Vieux Carre, the present-day French Quarter of New Orleans.

During the first half of the eighteenth century, the French settlers became experts at transforming the natural bounty of their new land into delicious dishes. Heirs of a long tradition of carefully cooked and exquisitely served foods, it was perhaps only natural that these people would turn their talents toward developing a cuisine that at once reflected their thriftiness and skill in the kitchen and their love of good food.

THE INDIANS AND THE AFRICANS

Their way of life brought the French newcomers into contact with two groups that were to have significant influence on what would evolve into the Creole cuisine. One group was the Choctaw Indians, the native Americans who had lived in and around the southern sections of the Mississippi and its delta for hundreds of years. Living off the land, in harmony with nature, they discovered many of her secrets. Among these was the use of native herbs and spices.

The Choctaw shared this knowledge with the French around New Orleans. Of all the seasonings the Indians introduced the French to, none had the importance of dried and powdered sassafras leaves. When added to a stew or soup, the leaves acted as a thickener, producing as well a spicy, elusive flavor. The settlers soon discovered that if a dish to which the leaves were added was reboiled, the result was a stringy mass. Thus was born the term *file*, French for "to make into threads."

The second people who influenced Creole cooking were the Africans. Brought to plantations around New Orleans as slaves for the fields and homes, these people, primarily from central Africa, made three significant contributions to what would be Creole cuisine. Frist, the women cooked foods in iron pots, as had been the custom in Africa. These pots permitted long, slow cooking so essential to the preparation of many dishes that dominate Creole cuisine. Second, the Africans brought with them okra, a green vegetable that thickens hot liquids. The Bantu word for okra was *kingombo* – from this came the Creole term *gumbo*, applied to a stewlike soup that has been thickened with okra, with file powder, or with both. Related to okra is the third African contribution to Creole cuisine: a cooking method that blends herbs and vegetables with a base of stock to prepare stews and thick soups. This method was almost never used in France, and it was African cooks who contributed it to Creole cuisine.

THE SPANISH

For over half a century, until 1762, the French in New Orleans lived, worked, and cooked in splendid isolation, incorporating into their life-style – and their cuisine – elements of their native land, their new land, and African and Indian cookery methods and knowledge. In essence, though, these people were still French. It took the additional infusion of the Spaniards to make them Creole.

France ceded New Orleans and the French Caribbean islands to Spain in 1762. With this cession came the influence of Spanish nobility – and the beginnings of the Creole culture. Like their French counterparts, settlers in Spanish America were courtiers and grandees whose emigration had the encouragement and blessing of the Spanish king and his court. Proud and haughty, they were an appropriate addition to the already insular French population around New Orleans and in the Caribbean islands.

For the next forty years, the French and Spanish settlers mixed, producing an ethnic group known as Creoles. The Creoles, born in the New World but retaining the lifestyle and customs of the Old, were a romantic and elegant people. In the early 1800's, eight thousand Creole refugees from slave uprisings in the islands of Haiti and Martinique came to make their homes in that last bastion of Creole culture, New Orleans. With them, they brought a cuisine that while essentially the same as that of Creole Louisiana, included the red hot pepper, a vegetable indigenous to their former homes. This pepper was the final element needed to complete the basic structure of Creole cookery.

THE CREOLE CUISINE

Like the French and Spanish forebears of the Creole people, Creole cuisine reflected treasured Old World foods and cooking techniques adapted to the New World's foods. The French gave a delicate touch to food and a sharp sense of household economy to the cuisine. The Spanish gave a love of hotly seasoned foods and a tendency to mix meat and poultry together in the same dish serving this mixture with or over rice. Overlying this blending of French and Spanish cuisines was the seasoning skill of the Choctaw Indians and the infinite patience and ingenuity of African cooks. The result of these interminglings was Creole cuisine, one of the most unusual and palate-tempting cuisines to be found anywhere in the world.

Of all Creole dishes, perhaps the soups and stews are the best known. There are *gumbos*, of turkey, chicken, rabbit, fish, squirrel, crab, oyster, shrimp, ham, or any other meat animal available cooked with seasonings and greens. Gumbos are thickened with either okra, in which case they are simply called gumbos, or with file powder. Gumbos thickened with this powder are called file gumbos. There is also a much-famed *gumbo z'herbes*, a blend of twelve or more fresh greens, fresh crayfish, and seasonings.

Gumbos are an excellent example of the diverse influences on Creole cookery. The making of a soup or stew from mixtures of meat, fish, and poultry is Spanish . . . the blend of herbs and greens is an African technique. Also African is the use of a heavy iron pot in which to cook the mixture. The painstaking technique of preparation and the economy reflected in its ingredients are French. The sum total is Creole — and delicious!

Akin to gumbo and often confused with it is *jambalaya*. On first glance, jambalaya appears to be gumbo with rice added. In fact, jambalaya is a direct descendent of the classic Spanish dish, *paella*. Here too are found the household economics typical of the Creoles. Where the Old World Spaniards used huge chunks of fresh fish and shellfish to make paella, the thrifty French influence led to the use of smaller pieces of meat and poultry as well as fish and shellfish. In other words, a jambalaya is the perfect way to use up leftovers!

The Creoles not only developed dishes uniquely their own, they also developed specialized cooking methods. One is known as cooking *en papillote*: literally, in an envelope. Individual portions of poached fish, poultry, or meat are placed on one side of a piece of foil or parchment. A delicately flavored sauce is prepared and gently spooned on top of each portion. Usually, mushroom caps are added, and the foil or parchment is folded over to form an envelope that is then tightly sealed. The entire package is baked, and after baking, is served to the diner who cuts the envelope open and eats its contents.

Another Creole method of food preparation seals in juices. When meats are cooked separately from any other ingredients, special preparation methods are used. Meats to be fried or cooked in fat are seared in hot fat first to seal in their juices. By sealing in these juices, shrinkage and flavor loss is prevented. Similarly, meats to be cooked by moist-heat methods are first plunged into boiling water to sear them. Vegetables that are to be cooked by themselves are also seared in hot fat or are put into boiling water.

Critical to Creole cookery are its sauces, and the base of the sauces is the *roux*. This is a mixture of hot fat, usually butter, and flour that is cooked until the raw taste of the flour is gone and the color is golden brown.

The Creole cuisine took form about the early 1800's. It has altered remarkably little in the past two centuries since that time. Retaining its character despite pressures from the modern world around it, Creole cookery, like the Creole city of New Orleans, Vieux Carre, has stayed unchanged. Elegant and memorable — that is Creole cuisine.

cooking with

WINES AND SPIRITS

The careful use of spirits – wines and liquors – in foods was and still is characteristic of Creole cookery. It is as much a part of this cookery as the iron pot in which many dishes were prepared and the frugality and inventiveness of the Creole cooks. These women used spirits to enhance the flavor of a dish. They knew that the alcohol content in spirits would burn off during cooking, leaving only an elusive and delicious bouquet to tantalize the palate. Because the quality of this bouquet depended on the quality of the spirits used, only those wines and liquors considered good enough to drink were used in cooking. In other words, Creole cooks would have assiduously avoided what is referred to today as "cooking wines." In fact, cooking wines are residues that are closer in their chemical composition to vinegar than to fine table wines. By the same token, harsher tasting liquors would also have been avoided.

Whatever spirit a Creole homemaker decided to add to a dish, she would add it during cooking to allow the alcohol to completely evaporate and the bouquet to permeate the entire dish. When she added spirits after cooking, the spirit steeped the dish, creating both a richer bouquet and a stronger alcohol taste. In adding spirits to the Creole dishes you prepare, be guided by your personal preference as well as those of your family and guests in determining which method you will follow.

Among the liquors often used in Creole cooking were rum and bourbon both of which came to replace the brandy or cognac frequently used in France but hard to find in eighteenth and nineteenth century New Orleans. Ulti-

10

mately, wines were used in Creole cookery with far more frequency than liquors, as the chart that follows illustrates.

To help you determine which wines you might prefer to incorporate into a dish, here is a brief description of those mentioned: *Burgundy* is a dry (unsweetened), full-bodied red wine. Pinot Noir, Red Pinot, and Gamay are burgundies that are named for the grapes from which they came. *Chablis* is a dry, mildly tart and full-bodied white wine; the best known type is Pinot. *Chianti* is a dry, mildly tart, full-bodied red or white wine that was introduced into New Orleans by newcomers from Italy. *Claret* is a dry, tart, and light- to medium-bodied deep red dinner wine. Cabernet, Zinfandel, and Grignolino are popular clarets. *Dubonnet* is a very sweet, rich red or white wine. *Muscatel* is a fruit-flavored sweet wine with the distinct flavor and aroma of the Muscat grapes from which it is produced. *Port* is a rich, sweet, full-bodied, fruit-flavored wine that ranges in color from deep red to pale gold to tawny. *Rhine wines* are very dry, tart, light-bodied white wines; among the best known types are the Reislings. *Sauterne* is a gold colored, full-bodied white wine that may be dry or sweet. Types include Semillon, Sauvignon Blanc, and Haut Sauterne. *Sherry* is a rich, nut-flavored wine that ranges from dry to sweet and in color from pale to dark amber. There is also a cream sherry that is generally not suitable for cooking. *Tokay* is a pinkish amber wine with a slightly nutlike flavor. Like Muscatel, it has the flavor of the grapes from which it is produced. *Vermouth* is a spicy, aromatic, light-bodied wine that may be dry or sweet.

COURSE	COMPLEMENTARY SPIRITS
Cheese	Red wines, especially port
Desserts	Brandy, rum, white and red wines
Eggs	Brandy, rum
Fish	White wines, vermouth, fruit wines
Fruits	Cider, applejack, brandies, tawny port
Game, dark	Sherry, red wines, brandy, rum
Game, white	Dry white wines, fruit wines
Hors d'oeuvres	Sherry, Dubonnet, white wines
Meat	Burgundy, claret, port, bourbon
Oysters	White wines
Poultry	Burgundy, white port, rum, brandy
Salads	White and red wines
Shellfish	White wines, vermouth
Soups	Sherry, claret, burgundy
Vegetables	Sweet white wines, rum

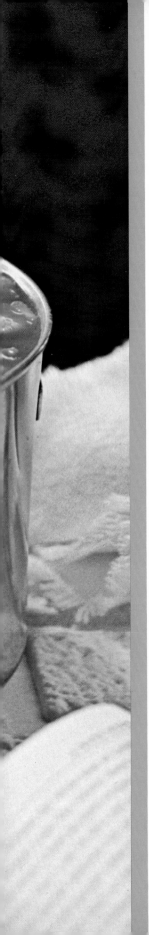

Bayou Gumbo (page 20)

creole soups and gumbos

The iron pot in which soups and gumbos were prepared was a permanent part of Creole households. It sat on the back of the stove all day long, making delicious stock from meat scraps and bones, vegetable scrapings and tops, and other food scraps. From this stock came the soups and gumbos that are so much a part of Creole cuisine. Although the stock pot is a thing of the past, the savory recipes that it contributed to are still very much a part of the Creole heritage. And the best, family-tested soup and gumbo recipes are yours in the pages that follow.

Begin by trying Bouillon, an elusively flavored soup you'll want to serve often. Discover recipes for Creole Stock Pot and Turtle Soup, both hearty enough to serve as the main dish at lunch or supper. There's even a hard-to-find recipe for Court Bouillon, the delicately-flavored soup in which Creoles poached their fish.

In this section soups are combined with page after page of gumbo recipes. Gumbos — more like rich stews than soups — are unique to the Creole cuisine. Treat your family to hearty Chicken Gumbo File, a filling gumbo thickened with the last-minute addition of powdered sassafras leaves known as file powder.

Imagine the pleasure you'll give family and friends by introducing them to Creole cooking through these delicious soups and gumbos. In fact, why not prepare one now?

CLASSIC BOUILLON

6 lb. meaty beef bones	2 tbsp. chopped parsley
4 qt. cold water	6 peppercorns
2 carrots, sliced	1 bay leaf
2 onions, sliced	2 tsp. salt
3 stalks celery with leaves, diced	

Crack the beef bones. Brown in small amount of fat in a large kettle. Add remaining ingredients. Bring to a boil and skim off foam from surface. Cover and simmer for 3 hours or until liquid is reduced by half. Remove bones, beef and vegetables. Strain the broth through cheesecloth and cool, then chill. May be served hot or cold.

Mrs. Faye Frazier, San Antonio, Texas

COMBINATION CONSOMME

3 lb. stewing beef	1/4 c. butter
3 lb. knuckle of veal	1 tsp. thyme
1 lb. marrow bone	1 sprig of marjoram
3 qt. cold water	2 sprigs of parsley
2 pt. chicken stock	1 bay leaf
1/2 c. diced carrots	4 cloves
1/2 c. diced turnips	1 tsp. peppercorns
1/2 c. diced celery	1 tsp. salt
1/2 c. diced onions	

Cut the beef and veal into small pieces. Brown half the beef in some of the marrow from the bone in a large kettle. Add bones, remaining meat and water and let stand for 30 minutes. Bring to boiling point slowly and simmer for 3 hours, removing scum as it forms. Add the chicken stock and simmer for 2 hours. Cook the carrots, turnips, celery and onion in a saucepan in butter for 5 minutes, then add to the beef mixture. Add the spices and seasonings and simmer for 1 hour and 30 minutes longer. Strain and cool. Remove fat carefully. Reheat and serve. 8-12 servings.

Mrs. Russell Carter, Mobile, Alabama

JELLIED VEAL CONSOMME

3 lb. veal knuckle or shin bones	2 bay leaves
Necks and wings of 2 chickens	2 sprigs of thyme
3 qt. water	2 cloves
1 tbsp. salt	1 onion
1/4 tsp. peppercorns	Dash of cayenne pepper
3 stalks celery	6 tbsp. minced pimento
	6 green pepper rings

Place the bones in a kettle with remaining ingredients except pimento and green pepper and cover. Heat to boiling point and skim off foam from surface. Simmer for 4 hours. Strain the broth through double thickness of cheesecloth, then chill until firm. Break up with a fork and place in 6 chilled bouillon cups. Place 1 tablespoon pimento in center of each cup and surround with green pepper rings.

Mary Ann Griffin, Panama City, Florida

CONSOMME MARIE WITH EGG PATTIES

2 cans consomme	1/2 lb. fresh mushrooms
1 sm. can asparagus tips	2 tbsp. chopped parsley
Salt and pepper to taste	Egg Patties
1 pkg. frozen green peas	

Pour the consomme into a large saucepan. Drain the asparagus and reserve liquid. Add enough water to reserved liquid to make 3 1/2 cups liquid and stir into the consomme. Bring to a boil and season with salt and pepper. Add the peas and bring to a boil. Slice the mushrooms thin and add to the saucepan. Cook until the peas are crisp-tender. Stir in the parsley. Cut the asparagus tips in half and place in 8 heated soup bowls. Ladle the mushroom mixture over asparagus. Serve with Egg Patties.

Egg Patties

1 pkg. frozen cream puff shells	Salt to taste
2 eggs	3 tbsp. ground almonds
1 egg yolk	3 tbsp. flour

Thaw the cream puff shells. Mix remaining ingredients in a heavy saucepan and simmer, stirring, until thick. Remove from heat and beat until cold. Place the egg mixture in the cream puff shells and place on a cookie sheet. Bake at 400 degrees until brown and heated through.

Consomme Marie with Egg Patties (above)

CREOLE STOCK POT

3 lb. lean beef chuck	4 green onions, tops removed
1 soupbone	3 stalks celery with leaves
1 1/2 tbsp. salt	2 lge. onions
1 tsp. crushed red pepper	2 ripe tomatoes
4 carrots	1 bouquet garni
2 turnips	2 whole cloves
1 parsnip	

Cut the chuck into 1-inch cubes and place in a kettle. Crack the soupbone and add to kettle. Add 3 quarts water, salt and pepper and bring to a boil. Remove foam from surface and reduce heat. Cover and simmer for 4 hours. Pare the carrots, turnips and parsnip and cut in large pieces. Clean the green onions and celery and slice. Peel and chop the onions and tomatoes. Add the vegetables, bouquet garni and cloves to the kettle and simmer for 1 hour and 30 minutes. Remove from heat. Strain the stock through a fine sieve and cool. Chill, then remove fat from top. Reheat to serving temperature. Stock may be used in other creole recipes.

Mrs. Lois Church, Oklahoma City, Oklahoma

MULLIGATAWNY

1 lge. onion, chopped	1/4 tsp. cayenne pepper
2 tbsp. margarine or oil	2 tbsp. instant flour
2 med. Winesap apples	4 c. chicken broth, heated
1 lge. carrot	Cooked rice
1 med. turnip	Flaked coconut
4 tomatoes	Seedless raisins
1/2 tbsp. curry powder	

Mulligatawny (above)

Fry the onion in the margarine in a large saucepan until tender. Peel and chop the apples, carrot, turnip and tomatoes. Add to the onion. Sprinkle with curry powder and cayenne pepper and cook for several minutes. Sprinkle with the flour and mix well. Add the broth and cook for about 10 minutes. Place 1 tablespoon rice in each soup bowl and add the soup. Serve with coconut and raisins.

LAMB-OKRA GUMBO

1 lb. ground lamb	2 cloves of garlic
2 med. onions, chopped	Salt and pepper to taste
1 med. green pepper, chopped	2 sm. packages frozen sliced
2 stalks celery, chopped	okra
1 lge. can tomatoes	1 lb. cleaned shrimp
3 bay leaves	

Place the lamb, onions, green pepper and celery in a kettle and cover with water. Bring to a boil, then reduce heat. Cover and simmer until the lamb is tender. Add the tomatoes, bay leaves, garlic, salt, pepper and okra and simmer for 2 hours, adding water as needed. Add the shrimp and cook for 30 minutes longer. Serve on rice.

Mrs. Frank Saunders, San Antonio, Texas

CHICKEN-OKRA GUMBO

1 fryer	1 can tomatoes
Salt and pepper to taste	1/4 bottle catsup
4 c. boiling water	1 8-oz. can tomato sauce
1 can cut okra, drained	1 lge. onion, chopped

Cut the fryer into serving pieces and season with salt and pepper. Cook in the water in a large saucepan until tender. Remove chicken from broth and cool. Remove chicken from bones and return to broth. Add remaining ingredients and bring to a boil. Reduce heat and simmer for 3 hours, stirring occasionally and adding water as needed. 8-10 servings.

Mrs. Joe Freeman, Shelby, North Carolina

OXTAIL SOUP

1 1 1/2-lb. oxtail	3/4 c. diced carrot
6 c. water	1/2 c. diced celery
1 tbsp. salt	2 tbsp. rice
1/2 c. diced onion	1 c. canned tomatoes

Cut the oxtail into 2-inch pieces and brown in small amount of fat in a kettle. Add the water and salt and bring to a boil. Reduce heat and cover. Simmer for 3 hours. Remove oxtail from broth and cool. Remove meat from bones and return meat to broth. Add the onion, carrots, celery, rice and tomatoes. Cover and simmer for 30 minutes longer. Skim off fat and serve. 6 servings.

Mrs. L. C. Davis, Durham, North Carolina

Jiffy Ripe Olive Chowder (below)

JIFFY RIPE OLIVE CHOWDER

2 tbsp. butter	1 tbsp. instant minced onion
2 tbsp. flour	1 7 1/2-oz. can corn
1 10 1/2-oz. can chicken	1 2 1/2-oz. can sliced
broth	ripe olives, drained
1 c. milk	1/8 tsp. fines herbes

Melt the butter in a large saucepan and blend in the flour. Stir in the chicken broth gradually. Add the milk and onion and cook, stirring, until mixture comes to a boil. Add the corn, olives and fines herbes and serve hot. About 3 cups.

CHICKEN GUMBO FILE

6 tbsp. shortening	2 tbsp. salt
6 tbsp. flour	2 tsp. pepper
1 onion, minced	1 green pepper, chopped
1/4 c. diced celery	1/2 c. chopped parsley
1 chicken	1/2 tsp. file powder

Place the shortening in a large saucepan and melt over high heat. Add the flour and stir constantly until dark brown. Add the onion and celery and stir until vegetables are wilted. Cut the chicken into serving pieces and add to saucepan. Add 6 cups hot water and mix well. Season with salt and pepper. Cover and simmer for about 1 hour and 30 minutes or until chicken is tender. Add the green pepper and parsley and simmer for 5 minutes. Remove from heat and add the file. Do not cook after file is added. Serve over rice.

Mrs. Stan Madison, Columbia, South Carolina

CORN AND CHICKEN CHOWDER

1/4 c. diced salt pork	2 c. chicken stock
1 med. onion, chopped	2 No. 2 cans cream-style corn
2 celery stalks, chopped	1 c. cubed cooked chicken
2 tbsp. chopped parsley	1 c. milk or cream
2 tbsp. flour	Crackers

Fry the salt pork in a large saucepan until crisp and remove from saucepan. Saute the onion, celery and parsley in fat in the saucepan until tender. Add the flour and blend well. Add chicken stock and bring to a boil, stirring constantly. Add corn and chicken and simmer for 10 minutes. Add the milk and simmer for 5 minutes longer. Serve piping hot over crackers crushed in soup bowls. 8 servings.

Mrs. Robert Lambert, Bowling Green, Kentucky

DUCK AND OYSTER GUMBO

2 ducks	2 tbsp. pepper sauce
1 c. cooking oil	Cayenne pepper to taste
1 c. flour	1 pt. oysters
1 lge. onion, chopped	Chopped parsley
Salt and pepper	Chopped onion tops
2 qt. warm water	

Cut the ducks into serving pieces. Heat the oil in a kettle. Add the flour and cook, stirring constantly, until brown. Add the onion and cook until tender, stirring occasionally. Season the ducks well with salt and pepper. Place in the kettle and cook until brown on all sides. Add the water and mix well. Simmer for about 2 hours or until ducks are tender. Season with salt and pepper to taste, pepper sauce and cayenne pepper. Add the oysters and cook for 20 minutes longer. Garnish with parsley and onion tops.

Mrs. Sarah Harris, Alexandria, Virginia

WILD DUCK GUMBO

3 tbsp. shortening	Salt and pepper to taste
3 tbsp. flour	3 c. water
1 med. onion, chopped	1 wild duck, disjointed
1 clove of garlic, minced	1 tsp. gumbo file
1 stalk celery, chopped	

Melt the shortening in a saucepan. Add the flour and cook until golden brown. Add the onion, garlic, celery, salt and pepper and cook until onion is tender. Add water and duck and cover. Cook until duck is tender. Add the gumbo file and remove from heat. Serve with rice, if desired. 2 servings.

Mrs. Jonas Hill, Prairieville, Louisiana

BAYOU GUMBO

4 tbsp. butter	1 bay leaf
4 tbsp. flour	1 1/2 tsp. thyme
2 lge. onions, chopped	2 lb. peeled deveined shrimp
2 cloves of garlic, minced	1 pt. oysters
1 can tomatoes, sieved	Salt and pepper to taste
1 can tomato paste	Hot sauce to taste
1 can consomme	1 1/2 tsp. file powder
4 consomme cans water	

Melt the butter in a kettle over low heat. Stir in the flour and blend well. Add the onions and garlic and cook until brown. Stir in the tomatoes, tomato paste, consomme and water and bring to a boil. Reduce heat. Add the bay leaf and thyme and simmer for 1 hour. Add the shrimp, oysters, salt, pepper and hot sauce and bring to a boil. Reduce heat and simmer for 15 minutes. Remove from heat and stir in the file powder. 8 servings.

Photograph for this recipe on page 12.

MACARONI GUMBO

1 7 3/4-oz. can crab meat	1 1-lb. 12-oz. can tomatoes
2 cloves of garlic, crushed	1 qt. water
1 c. chopped onions	1 pt. clam juice
1/4 c. butter or margarine	1 tbsp. salt

Macaroni Gumbo (above)

1 tsp. oregano leaves	1 10-oz. package frozen
2 bay leaves	baby okra
Dash of hot sauce	1 pt. shucked oysters, drained
2 c. elbow macaroni	1 lb. shelled shrimp, deveined

Drain the crab meat and remove cartilage. Saute the garlic and onions in butter in a Dutch oven or large heavy saucepan until golden. Add the tomatoes, water, clam juice, salt, oregano, bay leaves and hot sauce and simmer, covered, for 40 minutes. Bring to a boil and add the macaroni gradually. Add the okra and cook, covered, for 15 minutes or until macaroni is tender, stirring occasionally. Stir in the oysters, shrimp and crab meat and cook for 5 minutes longer. 6-8 servings.

SEAFOOD GUMBO

1 doz. oysters and liquor	1 tsp. salt
1 slice salt pork	1 bay leaf
1/2 sm. package frozen sliced	1/2 tsp. garlic salt
okra	Dash of pepper
1 onion, chopped	Dash of cayenne pepper
2 tbsp. flour	1 can crab meat, drained
2 c. canned tomatoes	1 lb. cleaned shrimp
6 c. boiling water	1 tbsp. file powder
2 sprigs of parsley	

Drain the oysters and reserve liquor. Fry the salt pork in a skillet until crisp. Remove from skillet and cut into small pieces. Saute the okra in drippings in the skillet until light brown. Add the onion and fry until tender, stirring constantly. Push vegetables to one side of skillet. Brown flour in the skillet. Stir in the onion and okra. Add the tomatoes, reserved liquor, boiling water and seasonings and stir until smooth. Simmer for 1 hour. Add salt pork, crab meat and shrimp and simmer for 5 minutes. Add the oysters and heat until edges of oysters curl. Do not boil. Remove from heat and add file. 6 servings.

Annie G. Childress, Mangham, Louisiana

CRAB GUMBO

4 slices bacon, diced	1 can tomato sauce
2 pkg. frozen sliced okra	1 bay leaf
2 stalks celery, diced	1/8 tsp. ground cloves (opt.)
2 med. onions, diced	1/8 tsp. rosemary leaves (opt.)
3 cloves of garlic, diced	2 tbsp. Worcestershire sauce
2 tbsp. chopped parsley	Salt and pepper to taste
1 lge. can tomatoes	1 lb. crab meat

Cook the bacon in a kettle until crisp, stirring constantly. Place the okra in bacon grease and cook over low heat until the okra is thawed, stirring occasionally. Add the celery, onions, garlic and parsley and cook for about 5 minutes. Add tomatoes, tomato sauce and 1 quart water and mix well. Add the bay leaf, cloves, rosemary and Worcestershire sauce and simmer for 1 hour. Add the salt, pepper and crab meat and cook for 15 minutes longer. Serve with rice.

Mrs. R. L. Falkenhagen, Galveston, Texas

CRAB BISQUE

1 can tomato soup	1/2 c. cream
1 can pea soup	Salt and pepper to taste
2 c. beef broth	2 tbsp. sherry (opt.)
1/2 lb. crab meat, flaked	

Mix the soups and broth in a saucepan and bring to a boil. Add the crab meat and cream and mix. Season with salt, pepper and sherry and heat through. Keep hot over low heat. 6 servings.

Mrs. Edgar Webb, Los Angeles, California

CRAWFISH BISQUE

1 lb. cleaned crawfish tails	1/2 c. minced onion
1/4 c. margarine	2 green onions, minced
1/4 c. flour	1/4 c. chopped carrot
1 tsp. salt	1 bay leaf
1/8 tsp. pepper	2 egg yolks, slightly beaten
5 c. chicken broth	1 c. cream
Hot sauce to taste	

Chop the crawfish tails. Melt the margarine in a kettle over low heat. Add the flour, salt and pepper and stir until smooth. Add the broth gradually and cook, stirring constantly, until mixed. Add the hot sauce, vegetables and bay leaf and cover. Simmer for 10 minutes. Add the crawfish and cover. Simmer for 10 minutes, then remove the bay leaf. Drain the crawfish and vegetables and reserve liquid in the kettle. Place crawfish mixture in a blender container and blend well. Place in reserved liquid and heat through. Stir 1/4 cup soup into egg yolks, then stir back into soup. Cook for 5 minutes, stirring constantly. Do not boil. Stir in the cream and heat through. 8 servings.

Mrs. Bert Newman, Cumberland, Maryland

OYSTER SOUP

2 qt. oysters	1/2 tsp. pepper
2 tbsp. hot water	2 tbsp. butter
1/2 tsp. salt	1 qt. scalded milk

Drain the oysters and reserve liquid. Mix reserved liquid and water and pour into a saucepan. Heat to boiling point. Add the salt, pepper and oysters and cook for 5 minutes. Stir in the butter and cook for 1 minute. Add the milk and bring to a boil, stirring constantly. Remove from heat and serve.

Mrs. Y. B. Hall, Galax, Virginia

OYSTER STEW

1 c. chopped celery	1/2 c. water
1/2 c. chopped green onions and tops	3 c. milk
	1/4 c. butter or margarine

1 tsp. salt	1 tbsp. flour
1/4 tsp. pepper	2 tbsp. chopped pimento
1 pt. oysters, drained	

Cook the celery and onions in water in a saucepan until water has evaporated. Scald the milk in a heavy saucepan, stirring constantly. Add celery, onions, butter, seasonings and oysters and cook over low heat for about 10 minutes or until oysters are heated through. Mix the flour with small amount of cold water and stir into oyster mixture. Cook until slightly thickened. Add pimento and mix. 4 servings.

Mrs. B. E. Carr, Birmingham, Alabama

TANGY JAMBALAYA

1 lb. fresh or frozen shrimp	1/2 c. chopped green pepper
2 qt. boiling water	1 10-oz. package frozen
2 California lemon slices	corn, partially thawed
2 sprigs of celery tops	2 med. tomatoes, chopped
2 tsp. salt	2 tsp. freshly grated lemon
2 c. sliced okra	peel
6 tbsp. butter or margarine	4 tbsp. freshly squeezed lemon
1 med. onion, finely chopped	juice

Partially thaw shrimp, if frozen. Add the shrimp to boiling water, seasoned with lemon slices, celery tops and salt, and simmer for 5 minutes. Drain the shrimp, then shell and devein. Saute the okra in 3 tablespoons butter in a large skillet, stirring frequently, until lightly browned. Add remaining butter, onion, green pepper and corn and saute until onion is tender. Add the shrimp, tomatoes, lemon peel and lemon juice and bring to a boil. Reduce heat and simmer for 2 to 3 minutes. Serve immediately. 4 servings.

Tangy Jambalaya (above)

23

Salmon Gumbo (below)

SALMON GUMBO

1 10-oz. package frozen sliced okra	2 c. hot water
1/3 c. bacon drippings	1 1-lb. can stewed tomatoes
1 c. chopped green onions with tops	Salt to taste
	1/4 tsp. pepper
1 c. diced celery	1 bay leaf
1/2 c. diced green pepper	6 drops of hot sauce
1 clove of garlic, minced	1 1-lb. can salmon
1/4 c. flour	1 1/3 c. cooked rice

Thaw the okra and saute in the bacon drippings in a large saucepan for 10 minutes or until okra appears dry, stirring occasionally. Add the onions, celery, green pepper and garlic and cook for about 5 minutes longer. Stir in the flour. Add the hot water and cook, stirring constantly, until slightly thickened. Add the tomatoes, salt, pepper and bay leaf and cover. Simmer for 20 minutes, then discard the bay leaf. Add the hot sauce. Remove bones from the salmon and add salmon to the gumbo. Heat through. Place the rice in 4 soup bowls and fill bowls with gumbo.

BOUILLABAISSE

1 whole redfish	1 bouquet garni
1 whole red snapper	Salt and pepper to taste
1 whole blackfish	Powdered dill to taste
1 whole sheepshead	Powdered thyme to taste

Olive oil
1 doz. cleaned hard-shelled
  crabs
4 lb. unpeeled shrimp
6 lb. unpeeled crawfish tails
1 pt. white wine

6 peeled tomatoes, chopped
1 clove of garlic, chopped
1 c. chopped green onions
1/2 tsp. saffron
Toasted garlic French bread
  slices

Remove heads of all the fish and place in a kettle. Add 1 quart water and the bouquet garni and bring to a boil. Reduce heat and simmer until liquid is reduced to 1 pint. Strain the stock and set aside. Discard fish heads. Slice the fish into steaks and sprinkle with salt, pepper, dill and thyme. Rub with small amount of olive oil and set aside. Place the crabs, shrimp and crawfish tails in a kettle and add the fish stock and wine. Simmer for 5 to 10 minutes or until shellfish are pink. Drain and reserve stock. Place shellfish on a platter. Fry the fish steaks in small amount of olive oil in a heavy skillet until brown, turning once. Remove from skillet and place on a platter. Add the tomatoes, garlic, green onions and reserved stock to the skillet and simmer for 5 minutes. Mix the saffron with small amount of liquid from skillet and spread over fish steaks. Pour the tomato mixture into a tureen. Serve the fish, shellfish and soup with French bread.

Mrs. T. M. Blackmon, Memphis, Tennessee

FISH STOCK

1 qt. water
1 tbsp. salt

1 lb. fish head, bones, skin
  and tail

Place all ingredients in a saucepan and bring to a boil. Reduce heat and cover. Simmer for 30 minutes. Strain liquid and chill.

Mrs. Dorothy Fields, Jackson, Mississippi

COURT BOUILLON

2 tbsp. butter
1 onion, chopped
1 green pepper, chopped
1 clove of garlic, chopped
1 can chopped mushrooms,
  drained
3 tbsp. flour
1 can tomatoes, mashed
1 can tomato paste
2 c. water

1 c. vinegar
1 lemon, sliced
1/4 tsp. powdered thyme
1/4 tsp. basil
1/4 tsp. allspice
2 bay leaves
Salt to taste
Hot sauce to taste
1 c. white wine
3 1/2 lb. red snapper fillets

Melt the butter in a kettle. Add the onion, green pepper, garlic and mushrooms and saute until onion is clear. Add the flour and stir until browned. Add the tomatoes, tomato paste, water, vinegar, lemon and seasonings and simmer for 1 hour. Add the wine and bring to a boil. Place the snapper in the sauce and cook for 10 minutes. Remove the bay leaves. Serve the snapper on rice and pour the sauce over snapper.

Audrey Allen, Charleston, West Virginia

TURTLE SOUP

1 soft-shelled turtle	2 tbsp. flour
4 qt. boiling water	1 can tomatoes, sieved
2 onions, chopped	Salt to taste
6 whole cloves	1 lemon, sliced
1 tsp. ground allspice	2 hard-boiled eggs, sliced
5 tbsp. butter	1/4 c. cream

Clean the turtle and cut into small pieces. Place in a kettle and add the water. Add onions and cloves and cook until turtle is tender. Add the allspice. Melt 2 tablespoons butter in a skillet. Add the flour and brown. Add some of the turtle broth, stirring constantly. Add tomatoes and cook for 30 minutes. Add the salt. Place the lemon, remaining butter, eggs and cream in a tureen and add the soup. Serve at once.

Mrs. A. W. Noland, St. Francisville, Louisiana

ONION SOUP

Butter	1/8 tsp. cayenne pepper
5 med. onions, sliced thin	1/8 tsp. pepper
6 c. bouillon	6 slices French bread
1/2 tsp. salt	1/4 c. grated Parmesan cheese

Melt 3 tablespoons butter in a large saucepan. Add the onions and cook, stirring frequently, until golden brown. Add the bouillon, salt, cayenne pepper, and pepper and bring to a boil. Cover and simmer for 15 minutes. Place the bread on a cookie sheet and toast on one side. Turn and spread with butter. Sprinkle with cheese and toast until cheese is melted. Pour the soup into 6 soup bowls and place 1 slice bread on soup in each bowl. Serve with additional cheese.

Mrs. Otis Campbell, Waco, Texas

KIDNEY BEAN SOUP

3 slices bacon, diced	2 c. hot water
1 onion, sliced	1 can red kidney beans
3 stalks celery, diced	2 slices lemon
2 bay leaves	1/2 tsp. salt
1 tbsp. flour	Pepper to taste
1 tsp. paprika	1 tsp. Worcestershire sauce

Cook the bacon, onion and celery in a saucepan until onion is tender. Add the bay leaves and flour and stir until smooth. Add the paprika, hot water, kidney beans, lemon, salt, pepper and Worcestershire sauce and cook for 20 minutes. Press through a coarse sieve and place back in saucepan. Heat through. Serve with croutons, if desired.

Mrs. Carl Bentley, Austin, Texas

Mushroom Soup with Ham (below)

MUSHROOM SOUP WITH HAM

1 hambone	1 tsp. salt
2 qt. water	1/4 tsp. pepper
2 stalks celery	1/2 lb. mushrooms, sliced
1 lge. onion	2 tbsp. butter or margarine
1 bay leaf	1 tbsp. minced parsley
1 can cream of mushroom soup	2 tsp. prepared mustard
1 c. rice	

Place the hambone in a large saucepan and add the water, celery, onion and bay leaf. Cover and simmer for 2 hours. Strain and skim the broth. Pour back into the saucepan. Trim lean meat from the bone. Cut in small pieces and return to broth. Stir in the soup, rice, salt and pepper and bring to boiling point. Stir and cover. Reduce heat and simmer for 20 minutes. Saute the mushrooms in butter until tender and add to the soup. Add the parsley and mustard and blend well. 6 servings.

CREME VICHYSSOISE

4 green onions, chopped	4 chicken bouillon cubes
1 med. onion, chopped	4 c. coffee cream
6 tbsp. butter	Salt and pepper to taste
4 med. potatoes, quartered	1 pt. sour cream

Cook the onions in butter in a kettle until tender. Add the potatoes, 4 cups water and bouillon cubes and boil for 30 minutes. Mash. Add the coffee cream, salt and pepper and bring to a boil. Cool. Add the sour cream and chill. 6 servings.

Mrs. Earl Ellis, New Summerfield, Texas

Green Goddess Salad (page 42)

creole salads

Living in the hot and humid climate of southern Louisiana and the Mississippi Delta, Creole families soon came to appreciate the cooling, appetite-lifting aspect of salads. They used locally grown fruits, fish, shellfish, and meats to create salads that appealed as much to the diner's eye as to his appetite. Their recipes for these salads became an important part of Creole cookery.

Picture yourself serving Stuffed Honeydews on a summer's evening. These colorful salads are a pleasing prelude to dinner or can end that meal on a light and cool note. The recipe for this easy-to-prepare salad is just one of the many recipes awaiting you in the pages that follow. Two more are for Creole adaptations of classic French salads — Asparagus Vinaigrette and Salad Nicoise. Both are tantalizingly flavored salads certain to bring you requests for "Seconds, please."

Explore the whole wonderful range of salads with Creole flavors: New Orleans Bean Salad . . . Creole Potato Salad . . . Wild Rice and Turkey Salad . . . and many more. And if you'd like to introduce a note of unusual Creole elegance to your table, feature a beautifully shimmering molded salad. Veal Mold and Molded Lamb Salad are just two such recipes you'll discover in this section.

Make meals in your home the same kind of adventure you'd experience in Old New Orleans. Begin a meal with one of these elegant, Creole-style salads.

Gingered Apple Chutney (below)

GINGERED APPLE CHUTNEY

2 3-oz. packages lemon gelatin	1 env. unflavored gelatin
3 1/2 c. ginger ale	3/4 c. mayonnaise
1 c. chutney	1/4 tsp. salt
2 c. finely chopped Washington Delicious apples	3/4 c. sour cream
	1 egg white, stiffly beaten
	1/4 c. chopped nuts

Dissolve the lemon gelatin in 3 cups ginger ale over hot water and chill until slightly thickened. Add the chutney and apples. Pour 2/3 of the mixture into an 8-cup mold and chill until firm. Soften the unflavored gelatin in remaining ginger ale and dissolve over hot water. Cool. Stir in the mayonnaise, salt and sour cream and chill until partially set. Fold in the egg white and nuts and spoon over congealed apple mixture. Chill until firm. Pour remaining apple mixture over the sour cream mixture and chill until firm. Unmold onto a platter and garnish with slices of apple dipped in lemon juice, if desired.

FRUIT PLATE AND DRESSING

2 eggs, beaten	1 c. miniature marshmallows
3 tbsp. sugar	1 c. chopped pecans
1 tbsp. cream	Pear halves
3 tsp. dry mustard	Peach halves
1/2 tsp. salt	Cantaloupe slices
3 tbsp. lemon juice	Pineapple rings
2 c. whipped cream	Bananas

Combine the eggs, sugar, cream, mustard, salt and lemon juice in top of a double boiler and cook over boiling water until thick, stirring constantly. Cool. Fold in the whipped cream, marshmallows and pecans. Arrange the fruits on a platter and serve dressing over fruits.

Mrs. Frances Morton, Tallulah, Louisiana

CRANBERRY SALAD

1 c. ground cranberries	1 c. boiling water
1 c. sugar	1 c. crushed drained pineapple
1 sm. package lemon gelatin	1/2 c. chopped nuts

Mix the cranberries and sugar in a bowl and let stand for several hours. Dissolve the gelatin in boiling water in a bowl and chill until partially set. Add the cranberry mixture, pineapple and nuts and mix. Pour into a mold and chill until firm. Serve on lettuce and garnish with mayonnaise. 4 servings.

Mildred Mixon, East Point, Georgia

STUFFED HONEYDEWS

3 honeydew melons	1 c. pineapple chunks
1 c. watermelon balls	1 c. mandarin orange sections
1 c. cantaloupe balls	1 1/2 c. port
1 c. honeydew balls	

Cut 1 inch off top of each melon and scoop out seeds. Combine the fruits and place in melon cavities. Pour 1/2 cup port over fruit in each melon and replace tops of melons. Chill for 2 to 3 hours. Cut melons into halves to serve. 6 servings.

Mrs. R. M. Patrick, Columbia, South Carolina

FRESH STRAWBERRY SALAD

2 pt. fresh strawberries	1 1/2 c. boiling water
Sugar to taste	1 lge. can crushed pineapple
2 sm. packages strawberry gelatin	1 carton sour cream

Hull and slice the strawberries and add sugar. Dissolve the gelatin in water in a bowl, then cool. Add the pineapple and strawberries and mix well. Pour half the mixture into a mold and chill until set. Spread the sour cream over congealed mixture. Cover with remaining gelatin mixture and chill until firm.

Sibyl Bateman, New Orleans, Louisiana

WATERMELON DELIGHT

1 sm. package cherry gelatin	2 c. watermelon balls

Prepare the gelatin according to package directions, using 1 3/4 cups water, and refrigerate until partially set. Stir in the watermelon balls and chill until firm. 5 servings.

Mrs. Merle Smith, Lynchburg, Virginia

ARTICHOKE SALAD

1 9-oz. package frozen artichoke hearts	3 tbsp. mayonnaise
8 c. torn mixed salad greens	1/2 c. diced pared cucumber
1/2 c. sliced radishes	1 tbsp. lemon juice
2 tbsp. herb-seasoned croutons	1/2 tsp. garlic salt
1/3 c. buttermilk	1/2 tsp. sugar
	1/8 tsp. pepper

Cook the artichoke hearts according to package directions and drain. Chill. Place the greens in a large bowl and arrange artichoke hearts and radish slices over greens. Sprinkle with croutons. Blend the buttermilk and mayonnaise in a bowl until smooth and stir in the cucumber and lemon juice. Add remaining ingredients and mix. Drizzle half the dressing over salad and toss lightly. Serve salad with remaining dressing.

Mrs. Bob Warner, Annapolis, Maryland

ASPARAGUS VINAIGRETTE

1 tsp. sugar	1/4 c. sweet pickle relish
1 1/2 tsp. salt	2 tbsp. chopped parsley
1/8 tsp. cayenne pepper	1/4 c. chopped green pepper
1/4 tsp. paprika	2 tbsp. chopped pimento
Dash of garlic juice	1 tbsp. capers
1/3 c. vinegar	2 lge. cans asparagus, drained
1 c. salad oil	
1/4 c. chopped green onion	

Combine the sugar, salt, cayenne pepper, paprika and garlic juice in a bowl. Add the vinegar and salad oil slowly, beating constantly. Add the onion, relish, parsley, green pepper, pimento and capers and mix well. Pour over asparagus in a bowl and refrigerate overnight. 4-6 servings.

Mrs. H. M. Jones, Dover, Delaware

AVOCADO MOLD

1 1/2 env. unflavored gelatin	2 dashes of hot sauce
1/2 c. cold water	2 1/2 c. sieved ripe avocados
3/4 c. boiling water	Green food coloring (opt.)
2 tbsp. lemon juice	1 c. sour cream
1 1/4 tsp. salt	1 c. salad dressing or mayonnaise
1 tsp. grated onion	

Soften the gelatin in cold water in a bowl, then stir in boiling water until dissolved. Add the lemon juice, salt, onion and hot sauce and mix well. Cool. Stir in the avocados, several drops of food coloring, sour cream and salad dressing and turn into a 6-cup mold. Chill until firm. Unmold and garnish with watercress.

Mrs. Ruth Parkman, Ft. Worth, Texas

FRENCH AVOCADO SALAD

2 ripe avocados
Lemon juice
3 strips bacon

1/2 c. French dressing
4 romaine leaves

Cut the avocados into halves. Remove seeds and peel. Brush lemon juice on cut surfaces. Fry the bacon in a skillet until crisp, then drain and crumble. Mix with the French dressing and pour into cavity of each avocado half. Serve on romaine leaves.

Mrs. Thomas Place, Winston-Salem, North Carolina

CALIFORNIA AVOCADO RIBBON LOAF

2 1/4 c. tomato juice
1 6-oz. package lemon
   gelatin
3 tbsp. lemon juice
1 tbsp. horseradish
1/4 c. chopped green onions
1 4 1/2-oz. can med. shrimp,
   drained

1/3 c. boiling water
2 peeled California avocados,
   mashed
1/2 c. sour cream
1/2 tsp. seasoned salt
Lettuce
California avocado slices

Pour the tomato juice into a saucepan and heat to boiling point. Reserve 1/4 cup gelatin. Dissolve remaining gelatin in the tomato juice and stir in 2 tablespoons lemon juice and the horseradish. Chill until syrupy. Add the onions and shrimp. Spoon 1/2 of the mixture into a loaf pan and chill until firm. Dissolve reserved gelatin in boiling water in a bowl and stir in remaining lemon juice, mashed avocados, sour cream and salt. Spread over firm gelatin and chill until firm. Top with remaining tomato mixture and chill until firm. Serve on lettuce-lined platter and garnish with avocado slices. 8 servings.

California Avocado Ribbon Loaf (above)

CAESAR SALAD

1 clove of garlic, pressed	1/4 c. lemon juice
1/2 c. salad oil	1 egg, beaten
1 head lettuce	1/2 c. grated Parmesan
1 bunch curly endive	cheese
4 tomatoes, diced	1/4 c. crumbled bleu cheese
1 c. croutons	1 tsp. Worcestershire sauce
1 2-oz. can anchovy	1/2 tsp. pepper
fillets, drained (opt.)	1/2 tsp. salt

Combine the garlic and salad oil and let stand for at least 1 hour. Tear the lettuce and endive into bite-sized pieces and place in a salad bowl. Add the tomatoes, croutons and anchovies and mix. Strain the oil mixture and pour over lettuce mixture. Combine remaining ingredients and beat well. Pour over the salad and toss lightly. Yield: 6 servings.

Shirley Ann Murray, Winchester, Virginia

ELEGANT GREEN BEAN SALAD

1 lb. fresh green beans	Freshly ground pepper
2 tsp. salt	Dash of cayenne pepper
1/2 c. salad oil	1 hard-cooked egg yolk,
1/2 c. lemon juice	riced
1 tsp. dry mustard	2 tbsp. capers

Wash the beans and snap ends, pulling away strings. Leave beans whole. Pour 1 inch of water into a large saucepan and bring to a boil. Add beans and 1 teaspoon salt and cook for 5 minutes. Cover; and reduce heat. Simmer for 10 minutes, then drain. Combine the oil, lemon juice, remaining salt, mustard, pepper and cayenne pepper. Place the beans in a large bowl and pour dressing over beans. Mix lightly and cool. Cover and refrigerate for at least 2 hours. Drain the beans and arrange in bundles on salad plates. Garnish with egg yolk and capers.

Mrs. Mamie Booker, Pensacola, Florida

NEST EGGS

3 env. unflavored gelatin	1/2 tsp. dry mustard
1 c. tomato juice	1/8 tsp. white pepper
2 1/2 c. chicken broth	8 sprigs of fresh dill or
2 egg whites, slightly beaten	parsley
2 egg shells, crushed	1/2 c. shredded cabbage
4 hard-cooked eggs	1 carrot, grated
1/4 c. mayonnaise	1/4 c. chopped green pepper
2 tsp. prepared mustard	

Sprinkle the gelatin over the tomato juice in saucepan. Add the chicken broth, egg whites and shells and bring to a full boil, stirring constantly. Remove from heat and let stand for several minutes. Pour through a strainer lined with a towel or napkin that has been rinsed in cold water and rung out. Slice the eggs in half lengthwise and remove yolks, keeping whites intact. Place the yolks in a bowl and mash with a fork. Add the mustards and pepper and blend. Spoon into egg whites and chill. Place 1 tablespoon aspic in bottom of each of eight 6-ounce custard cups. Place 1 sprig of dill in each and chill until partially set. Spoon 2 tablespoons aspic into each cup and place 1/2 deviled egg, yellow side down, in each. Chill until partially set. Spoon 3 tablespoons aspic into each cup. Place vegetables in a ring around each egg and chill until partially set. Pour remaining aspic over vegetables to cover, allowing about 2 tablespoons for each cup, and chill until firm.

DIVIDEND DINNER

2 env. unflavored gelatin
2 1/2 c. cold water
3 beef bouillon cubes
1/2 c. tomato juice
2 tbsp. vinegar or lemon juice
2 c. julienne strips cooked
    beef or ham

1/2 c. sliced celery
1 c. cooked mixed vegetables
6 sm. radishes, sliced
1 1/2 c. diced cooked
    potatoes
1 tbsp. finely chopped onion

Sprinkle the gelatin over 1 cup water in a saucepan. Add the bouillon cubes. Place over low heat and stir constantly for 4 to 5 minutes or until gelatin and bouillon cubes are dissolved. Remove from heat and stir in remaining water, tomato juice and vinegar. Chill, stirring occasionally, until consistency of unbeaten egg white. Fold in remaining ingredients and turn into a 6-cup loaf pan or mold. Chill until firm. Unmold on a serving plate and garnish with parsley or salad greens and cherry tomatoes. 6 servings.

Top: Dividend Dinner (above)
Bottom: Nest Eggs (page 34)

NEW ORLEANS BEAN SALAD

1 can red kidney beans	1/4 tsp. salt
1/2 c. diced celery	Dash of pepper
2 tbsp. chopped dill pickles	1 tbsp. salad oil
2 tbsp. minced onion	1 tbsp. mild vinegar

Drain the beans and place in a bowl. Add remaining ingredients and toss lightly. Chill. Garnish with onion rings.

Mrs. Ruth Phillips, Mt. Pleasant, South Carolina

FRENCH BEAN SALAD

2 No. 2 cans French-style green beans	Dash of red pepper
	3 lge. onions, sliced thin
1 No. 2 can carrots	1 can tiny green peas, drained
1/4 c. vinegar	
1/2 c. sugar	1/2 bell pepper, chopped
3/4 c. salad oil	2 stalks celery, chopped
1 tsp. salt	

Drain the beans and carrots and place in a bowl. Mix the vinegar, sugar, oil, salt and pepper and mix with bean mixture. Cover with onions. Weight down with a plate and marinate at room temperature overnight. Add the peas, bell pepper and celery and refrigerate until chilled. Drain and serve with mayonnaise, if desired. 15 servings.

Mrs. Thomas E. Heaton, Decatur, Georgia

CREOLE POTATO SALAD

4 med. potatoes	2/3 c. water
1/4 lb. sliced bacon	1/3 c. vinegar
1/4 c. minced onion	1 egg, slightly beaten
2 tbsp. sugar	3/4 tsp. salt
2 tbsp. flour	

Cook potatoes in jackets in boiling, salted water until tender, then drain. Remove skins and cube potatoes while as hot as possible. Fry the bacon in a skillet until crisp. Remove from skillet and crumble. Drain all except 1/4 cup bacon drippings from skillet and heat. Add the onion and saute until golden. Stir in the sugar and flour and blend well. Reduce heat and stir in the water and vinegar. Add egg and salt and stir to blend. Cook for 1 minute. Add bacon and potatoes and mix gently to coat with dressing. Remove from heat and serve. 4 servings.

Mrs. George Veith, Louisville, Kentucky

SLAW WITH DRESSING

1 green cabbage, grated	1 c. finely chopped celery
Juice of 1 lemon	1 c. finely chopped green peppers
5 hard-boiled eggs, mashed	

1 c. finely chopped red
  peppers
1 tbsp. prepared mustard

3/4 c. mayonnaise
Salt and pepper to taste

Place the cabbage in a large bowl. Mix remaining ingredients. Add to cabbage and toss lightly. 15 servings.

Mrs. R. M. Boyney, McComb, Mississippi

VEGETABLE JUBILEE SALAD

1 3 to 4-oz. can chopped
  mushrooms
2 env. unflavored gelatin
2 c. water
Artificial sweetener
  equivalent to 4 tsp. sugar
1 tsp. salt
3/4 c. lemon juice

1/2 c. finely chopped green
  pepper
1/2 c. finely chopped cucumber
1/2 c. finely chopped radishes
1 c. finely chopped
  cauliflower
1 c. finely chopped celery

Drain the mushrooms and reserve liquid. Add enough water to reserved liquid to make 1/2 cup liquid. Pour into a saucepan and sprinkle with gelatin. Place over low heat and stir for about 3 minutes or until gelatin dissolves. Remove from heat and stir in the water, sweetener, salt and lemon juice. Chill until consistency of unbeaten egg whites, then fold in the vegetables. Turn into 2 sectioned ice cube trays with sections in place and chill until firm. Unmold and serve 3 or 4 cubes on individual lettuce-lined salad dishes. Cubes may be kept, covered, in refrigerator for snacking.

Vegetable Jubilee Salad (above)

TOMATO ASPIC CROWN

2 env. unflavored gelatin	1 tsp. Worcestershire sauce
3 1/4 c. tomato juice	1/4 tsp. hot sauce
1/2 tsp. salt	1/4 c. lemon juice
1 tsp. sugar	

Soften the gelatin in 1 cup tomato juice in a 2-quart saucepan. Place over moderate heat for 3 minutes or until gelatin is dissolved, stirring constantly. Remove from heat and stir in remaining tomato juice and remaining ingredients. Pour into 1-quart ring mold and chill until firm. Unmold and fill center with coleslaw, if desired. 6 servings.

Annette Ray, Falls Church, Virginia

SALADE DE RIZ

1 c. packaged precooked rice	1 sm. onion, diced
1 tomato, chopped	2 tbsp. mayonnaise
1 green pepper, diced	1 tsp. lemon juice
1 sm. cucumber, diced	Salt and pepper to taste

Cook the rice according to package directions, then cool and place in a bowl. Add remaining ingredients and mix well. Chill. Serve on lettuce. 4 servings.

Mrs. Elizabeth McKinley, Newport, Kentucky

HAM AND MACARONI SALAD

1 6-oz. package macaroni	2 tbsp. minced onion
2 c. diced cooked ham	Chopped green pepper to
1/4 lb. Cheddar cheese,	taste
diced	1/2 c. mayonnaise
1/4 c. diced sweet pickles	2 tbsp. mustard
2 tbsp. chopped pimento	1/4 tsp. salt

Prepare the macaroni according to package directions and drain. Place in a large bowl and chill. Add the ham, cheese, pickles, pimento, onion and green pepper and mix. Blend the mayonnaise with mustard and salt and stir into macaroni mixture. 6-8 servings.

Mrs. Raymond Boiland, Jonesboro, Louisiana

PORK AND APPLE SALAD

1 1/2 c. diced cooked pork	1/2 c. chopped pecans
2 c. diced apples	1/3 c. salad dressing
1 c. diced celery	1 tsp. salt

Combine the pork, apples, celery and pecans in a bowl and add the salad dressing and salt. Mix well and chill until serving time. Serve in lettuce cups. 6 servings.

Mrs. William Gilbert, Nashville, Tennessee

FLOUNDER SALAD

3/4 c. white wine	1 red pepper, sliced in rings
3/4 c. water	1 sm. package green peas,
1 1/2 tsp. salt	thawed
6 to 8 white peppercorns	1 green onion, sliced in
1 green onion, sliced	slivers
1 carrot, sliced	1 sm. jar pimento-stuffed
1 1/2 to 2 tsp. salad	olives
seasoning	1/4 c. French dressing
1 1-lb. package frozen	1/4 c. water
flounder fillets, thawed	3 tbsp. lemon juice
Dillweed	Dash of pepper
1 head iceberg lettuce	1 tbsp. chili sauce
1 cucumber, sliced	3/4 c. whipped cream

Mix first 7 ingredients in a saucepan and bring to a boil. Reduce heat and cover. Simmer for 15 minutes. Strain the liquid. Roll up the fillets and secure with picks. Place in a saucepan and cover with a thick layer of dillweed. Pour the strained liquid over the rolls and bring to a boil. Remove from heat and cool. Cover and chill. Drain the flounder rolls and cut in 1-inch pieces. Remove picks and place the rolls in a salad bowl. Shred the lettuce and place in the salad bowl. Add the cucumber, red pepper, peas and green onion. Drain the olives and cut in half. Add to the salad and toss lightly. Dilute the French dressing with the water in a jar and cover. Shake well. Pour over the salad and toss. Fold the lemon juice, pepper and chili sauce into the whipped cream in a bowl. Serve with the salad. 4 servings.

Flounder Salad (above)

SALADE NICOISE

5 tomatoes, quartered	2 hard-cooked eggs, quartered
1 sm. onion, thinly sliced	10 ripe pitted olives
1 green pepper, sliced in rings	1 c. drained chunk tuna
1/2 c. sliced radishes	1 clove of garlic, crushed
4 stalks celery, chopped	2 tbsp. wine vinegar
8 anchovy fillets	6 tbsp. oil
	Pinch of basil

Chill first 9 ingredients well. Place in a large salad bowl in order listed. Combine remaining ingredients in a jar and cover. Shake well. Pour over salad and toss lightly.

Mrs. Florence Yates, Chattanooga, Tennessee

VEAL MOLD

1 sm. veal shank	6 peppercorns
2 lb. veal	1 med. bay leaf
1 tsp. salt	1/2 c. diced celery
White pepper to taste	

Place the veal shank and veal in a kettle and cover with water. Bring to a boil and reduce heat. Simmer until veal is tender. Remove shank and veal from broth and cool. Remove veal from bone and discard bone. Grind veal coarsely. Strain the broth and pour back into the kettle. Add the veal, salt, white pepper, peppercorns, bay leaf, and celery and simmer until broth just covers veal. Remove the peppercorns and bay leaf. Pour into mold and chill until congealed. Remove to serving plate and garnish with parsley, olives and carrot curls. 8 servings.

Edith M. Anderson, Austin, Texas

MOLDED LAMB SALAD

2 sm. packages lemon gelatin	1/2 c. vinegar
2 c. boiling water	1/4 c. prepared horseradish
2 c. cold water	1 tbsp. salt
1/2 c. sliced olives	1/2 tsp. Worcestershire sauce
4 c. diced cooked lamb	
1/2 c. chopped green pepper	

Dissolve the gelatin in boiling water and stir in cold water. Make a design with some of the olives in a 5 x 9-inch pan and cover with thin layer of gelatin. Refrigerate until firm. Chill remaining gelatin until partially set. Stir in the lamb, green pepper, vinegar, horseradish, salt, Worcestershire sauce and remaining olives and pour over design in loaf pan. Chill until firm. Garnish with tomato slices. 10 servings.

Mrs. J. J. Brackin, Simmesport, Louisiana

WILD RICE AND TURKEY SALAD

1/2 lb. wild rice	1 c. diced celery
4 c. chopped cooked turkey	2 cans mandarin oranges,
1 c. mayonnaise	drained
1/2 c. French dressing	1 No. 2 can pineapple chunks,
Salt to taste	drained
1 5-oz. can sliced almonds	

Cook the rice according to package directions, then drain and cool. Add the turkey, mayonnaise, French dressing, salt, almonds and celery and mix well. Chill. Add oranges and pineapple just before serving and toss lightly. Serve on lettuce.

Mrs. Betty Nettles, Walterboro, South Carolina

GOLDEN FLOWER SALAD

1/2 c. sugar	2 cucumbers
1/2 c. vinegar	1 lge. stalk celery
3 Washington State Golden	Shredded lettuce
Delicious apples, unpared	1 c. small shrimp

Mix the sugar and vinegar. Quarter and slice the apples thin crosswise. Score the cucumbers with tines of a fork and slice into thin circles. Slice the celery slant-wise. Place the apples and vegetables in a bowl and pour the vinegar mixture over the apple mixture. Marinate for at least 1 hour in the refrigerator. Arrange full beds of lettuce on 6 individual salad plates. Drain the apple mixture. Arrange the cucumber slices in wide circle on lettuce. Place a circle of the apple slices, petal fashion, inside cucumber slices. Arrange the shrimp decoratively among the apples and place the celery in center for a flower effect. One cup cubed, cooked chicken may be substituted for the shrimp.

Golden Flower Salad (above)

CONSOMME-CHICKEN SALAD

1 env. unflavored gelatin	1/2 c. diced cooked chicken
1/2 c. cold water	1/2 c. minced cucumber
1 can consomme	1 tbsp. sliced stuffed olives
1/4 c. lemon juice	1 hard-cooked egg, chopped

Soften the gelatin in cold water. Heat 1/4 can consomme in a saucepan until hot. Add the gelatin and stir until dissolved. Add remaining consomme and lemon juice and chill until thickened. Fold in remaining ingredients and pour into a 1-quart mold. Chill until firm. Unmold and serve on salad greens. 6 servings.

Mrs. George Hill, Jr., Atlanta, Georgia

OYSTER SALAD

4 c. chopped poached oysters	1/4 tsp. pepper
1/3 c. minced celery	1/4 tsp. salt
1/4 c. minced parsley	1/3 c. French dressing
2 tbsp. finely chopped pimento	

Chill the oysters in a bowl. Add the celery, parsley, pimento, pepper, salt and French dressing and mix lightly. Serve on greens and garnish with tomato wedges, if desired. 4 servings.

Mrs. George Hunt, Little Rock, Arkansas

GREEN GODDESS SALAD

1 head iceberg lettuce	1/4 c. sour cream
1 bunch watercress	1 1/2 tbsp. anchovy paste
2 tomatoes, cut into wedges	1 1/2 tbsp. tarragon vinegar
1 med. onion, sliced	1 1/2 tsp. lemon juice
1/2 clove of garlic, crushed	3 tbsp. chopped parsley
1/2 c. mayonnaise	Lobster meat

Tear the lettuce into large pieces. Cut the watercress into small pieces. Place the lettuce, watercress and tomatoes in a bowl. Separate the onion slices into rings and add to the lettuce mixture. Chill. Blend the garlic with mayonnaise, sour cream and anchovy paste in a bowl, then stir in vinegar and lemon juice slowly. Add the parsley and chill. Pour dressing over the lettuce mixture and garnish with lobster meat. 6 servings.

Photograph for this recipe on page 28.

SHRIMP REMOULADE

4 hard-cooked eggs, minced	2 tbsp. finely chopped celery
1 c. mayonnaise	1 tsp. dry mustard
1 tbsp. anchovy paste	1/4 tsp. mashed garlic
2 tbsp. chopped parsley	1 tsp. Worcestershire sauce
2 tbsp. chopped green pepper	Salt and pepper to taste
2 tbsp. finely chopped onion	2 lb. jumbo shrimp

3 slices lemon
1 bay leaf
6 peppercorns

Pinch of thyme
Lettuce

Mix the eggs, mayonnaise, anchovy paste, parsley, green pepper, onion, celery, mustard, garlic, Worcestershire sauce, salt and pepper in a bowl and chill. Place the shrimp in a saucepan and cover with boiling, salted water. Add lemon, bay leaf, peppercorns and thyme and cook for about 10 minutes or until shrimp are done. Drain shrimp and cool. Shell and devein. Place shrimp on lettuce and serve mayonnaise mixture over shrimp. 4 servings.

Mrs. Ben Harrell, Fort Belvoir, Virginia

SHELLFISH SALAD

2 cans mussels in water
1 can lobster meat
1 sm. package frozen green
  peas

1 1/2 c. cold cooked rice
1 lb. cleaned cooked shrimp
Wine-vinegar dressing to
  taste

Drain the mussels and lobster meat. Thaw the peas. Place the rice in center of a salad bowl. Arrange the shrimp, mussels, peas and lobster meat around the rice. Add the dressing just before serving and toss. Serve with French bread and beer.

Shellfish Salad (above)

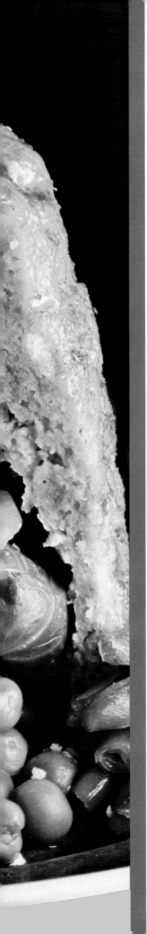

Stuffed Veal Timbale (page 52)

creole meats

Meats, carefully cooked with a touch of just-right seasonings and complemented with vegetables and accompaniments, formed the center of attraction at almost every Creole meal. The meat might be veal, lamb, pork, or beef. The cut could range from one of the many variety cuts to steaks, roasts, or chops. But whatever the meat and its cut, it was certain to be superbly prepared.

Many of the time-honored, home-tested recipes for preparing memorable meat dishes Creole-style have been gathered here in this section. Try veal in Creole Pilaf or French Rissoles, just two unusual and delicious ways to prepare this meat that is often a stranger at many American dinner tables. For those extra important meal occasions, feature Beef Bordelaise — beef cooked with palate-awakening seasonings.

Many Creole meat dishes combined two or more meats. Jambalaya, one of the most popular of the Creole meals in a dish, is such a combination. Tomato-rich, hotly-seasoned, this is an economical but flavor-packed main dish certain to bring compliments from everyone who enjoys it.

Bring the mouth-watering flavors of Creole-style meats to your family and guests by trying one of these home-tested recipes tonight. When you experience the new flavors waiting for you, you'll know why Creole cooking is considered one of the world's finest cuisines.

45

CREOLE DINNER

1/2 lb. sliced bacon	2 med. carrots, thinly sliced
1 lb. round steak	4 med. potatoes, thinly sliced
Salt and pepper to taste	1 c. cold water
3 med. onions, thinly sliced	

Place the bacon in a large skillet. Cut the steak crosswise into thin strips and place over bacon. Sprinkle with salt and pepper. Add the onions, then add the carrots. Sprinkle with salt and pepper. Add the potatoes and season with salt and pepper. Cook over low heat for 3 minutes. Add the water and cover the skillet. Simmer for 45 minutes. Canadian bacon may be substituted for bacon.

Mrs. Harrell Batte, Baton Rouge, Louisiana

CREOLE STEAK

1 lb. round steak	1 c. chopped onions
1/4 c. flour	1/3 c. chopped green pepper
2 tsp. salt	1/4 c. shortening
2 tsp. paprika	1/2 c. rice
1/2 tsp. pepper	2 1/2 c. canned tomatoes

Cut the steak into serving pieces. Mix the flour, salt, paprika and pepper, then dredge the steak in flour mixture. Reserve remaining flour mixture. Brown the onions and green pepper in shortening in a frypan and remove from frypan. Brown steak in remaining shortening and cover with the onion mixture. Sprinkle rice over onion mixture and cover with tomatoes. Sprinkle reserved flour mixture over the tomatoes and cover tightly. Simmer for 1 hour.

Mrs. Russell Barron, Lenox, Tennessee

STEAK WITH CARROTS

1 1-lb. round steak	6 lge. carrots
Salt and pepper to taste	1/2 lb. sliced bacon

Pound the steak well and season with salt and pepper. Slice the carrots lengthwise and place on the steak. Roll as for jelly roll. Place bacon slices around steak and tie in place. Brown steak in small amount of fat in a Dutch oven, then add small amount of water. Cover and cook over low heat for 1 hour or until tender. Slice and serve.

Mrs. Harold Monroe, Fort Lauderdale, Florida

GRILLADES AND GRAVY

1 round steak	1/2 c. minced onion
4 tbsp. shortening	1/2 c. chopped tomatoes
2 tbsp. flour	1 tsp. minced garlic

| 1 tbsp. minced green pepper | Salt and pepper to taste |
| 1 tbsp. minced parsley | |

Cut the steak in individual servings. Fry in a Dutch oven in the shortening until brown, then remove from Dutch oven. Brown the flour in the same shortening. Add the onion and cook until tender. Add the tomatoes, garlic, green pepper, parsley, salt and pepper. Add the steak and 2 cups water. Cover and cook over low heat for about 1 hour and 30 minutes or until tender. Serve with cooked rice.

Mrs. S. C. Taylor, Yuma, Arizona

COEUR DE FILET PROVENCALE

1 4 1/2-lb. beef tenderloin	1 clove of garlic, crushed
Salt	Finely chopped parsley to
Pepper to taste	taste (opt.)
3/4 c. butter	16 med. potatoes

Place the tenderloin in a baking pan and season with salt to taste and pepper. Bake at 325 degrees for about 1 hour and 15 minutes or until medium rare. Place the butter, garlic and parsley in a saucepan and cook until butter is light brown. Peel the potatoes and slice thin. Wash in cold water and dry on paper towels. Place the potatoes in a greased ovenproof dish in layers, seasoning each layer with salt, then cover with foil. Bake at same time along with tenderloin for 15 minutes. Remove the foil and pour 2/3 of the butter mixture over the potatoes. Bake for 25 minutes longer or until the potatoes are golden brown. Slice the tenderloin and keep slices together. Place on the potatoes and pour remaining butter mixture over the tenderloin. Increase oven temperature to 400 degrees and bake for 10 minutes longer.

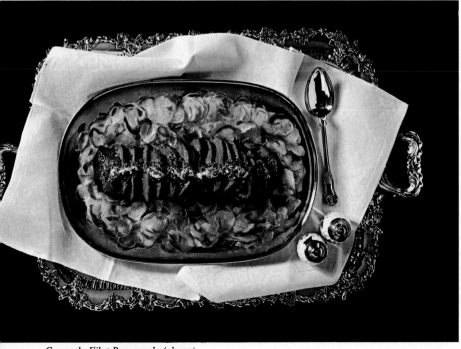

Coeur de Filet Provencale (above)

French Casserole with Red Wine (below)

FRENCH CASSEROLE WITH RED WINE

1/2 lb. sliced bacon, diced	Thyme to taste
2 1/2 lb. beef, cut in cubes	Red wine
1 or 2 bay leaves	1/2 lb. small onions, peeled
Salt and pepper to taste	3/4 lb. mushrooms

Fry the bacon in a skillet until brown, then remove from skillet. Drain off most of the fat. Add the beef to the skillet and cook until dark brown. Add the bacon, bay leaves, salt, pepper and thyme and place in a casserole. Add enough wine to cover, then cover with a lid. Bake at 300 degrees for 1 hour and 30 minutes. Brown the onions and mushrooms in small amount of bacon fat. Add to the beef mixture and cover. Bake for 30 minutes longer, adding wine, if needed. Thicken the gravy with cornstarch, if desired. Serve with rice and a green salad.

BOEUF BOURGUIGNONNE

1 c. red wine	6 tbsp. butter
1 tsp. parsley flakes	1 tbsp. flour
1 sprig of thyme	1/2 c. meat stock
1/2 bay leaf	1 lge. can button mushrooms
2 lb. lean stew beef	12 button onions
1 sliced onion	

Mix the wine, parsley, thyme and bay leaf in a bowl. Add the beef and marinate for 3 hours. Drain the beef and strain and reserve marinade. Cook the sliced onion in 4 tablespoons butter in a saucepan until golden. Add the beef and cook until brown. Remove beef and onion from saucepan. Stir the flour into drippings in saucepan and cook until brown. Stir in the meat stock slowly. Add reserved marinade, onion and beef and cover. Simmer for 3 hours. Drain beef and reserve liquid. Drain the mushrooms. Cook the button onions and mushrooms in remaining butter in a saucepan until golden. Place the beef on a platter and surround with onions and mushrooms. Heat reserved liquid and serve with the beef mixture. 4 servings.

Mrs. Russell Carter, Montgomery, Alabama

BARBECUED MEATBALLS

1/2 c. soft bread crumbs	2 tbsp. margarine
1/4 c. milk	1/4 c. molasses
1 lb. ground beef	1/4 c. vinegar
1 tsp. salt	1/4 c. catsup
1/2 tsp. monosodium glutamate	1/4 tsp. hot sauce
1 sm. onion, minced	1/2 tsp. marjoram
Flour	

Soak the bread crumbs in milk in a bowl for 5 minutes. Add the beef, salt, monosodium glutamate and onion and mix well. Shape into 12 balls. Roll in flour and brown in the margarine in a skillet. Stir in remaining ingredients and simmer for 10 minutes, stirring occasionally. 4 servings.

Carol Skinner, Elmore, Alabama

BEEF BORDELAISE

1 6-lb. rolled beef rump	5 sprigs of parsley
2 c. sliced onions	1 tsp. salt
1/2 c. chopped green onions	2 c. dry red wine
2 cloves of garlic, pressed	5 tbsp. melted butter
1 bay leaf	2 cans beef broth
1/2 tsp. crumbled leaf thyme	1 tbsp. flour
1 tsp. peppercorns	

Place the beef in a large container. Mix the onions, green onions, garlic, bay leaf, thyme, peppercorns, parsley, salt and wine and pour over beef. Cover and refrigerate for 12 hours, turning beef occasionally. Remove beef from marinade and pat dry. Strain and reserve the marinade and vegetables. Place the beef on a rack in a shallow baking pan. Bake at 475 degrees for 30 minutes, basting occasionally with 4 tablespoons butter. Reduce temperature to 400 degrees. Add reserved vegetables to pan and bake for 40 to 45 minutes longer, basting occasionally with pan drippings. Remove beef to a serving platter and let stand for 15 minutes. Bring pan drippings to a boil and cook for 1 minute. Remove fat and add reserved marinade. Bring to boiling point and cook until only several tablespoons are left. Add the broth. Blend remaining butter and flour and stir into broth mixture. Cook, stirring constantly, until thick and smooth. Strain and serve with beef. 8-10 servings.

Mrs. Beth James, Gainesville, Georgia

BEEF A LA MODE

1 4-lb. beef rump roast	2 sprigs of thyme
4 tbsp. butter	1/2 bay leaf
1/4 lb. salt pork, sliced thin	Salt and pepper to taste
10 sm. white onions	3 tbsp. red or white wine
5 carrots, quartered	2 tbsp. brandy
1 sm. calf's foot	4 c. water
3 sprigs of parsley	

Brown beef well on all sides in butter in a Dutch oven. Cut deep gashes in the beef and place the salt pork in the gashes. Surround beef with onions and carrots. Add calf's foot, parsley, thyme and bay leaf and season with salt and pepper. Pour in the wine, brandy and water and cover. Simmer for about 5 hours or until beef is tender. Remove beef from the Dutch oven and cut across the grain in thin slices. Arrange slices on a heated serving dish and garnish with onions, carrots and meat of calf's foot. Skim fat from gravy and pour several spoons of gravy on beef slices. Strain remaining gravy and serve with beef. 8-10 servings.

Mrs. Jack Lafayette, New Orleans, Louisiana

ROAST BEEF AU JUS

1 5-lb. standing prime rib roast	Salt and pepper to taste

Let roast stand at room temperature for at least 1 hour. Rub roast with salt and pepper and place, fat side up, in a shallow pan. Roast at 375 degrees for 1 hour, then turn off heat. Let roast cool in the oven without opening oven door. Reheat in oven at 375 degrees for 40 minutes. Roast will be brown and crisp on the outside and rare in the center. 10 servings.

Mrs. Otis Cappell, Florence, Alabama

SPANISH-STYLE ROAST BEEF

3 cloves of garlic, minced	3/4 c. chopped green pepper
1 1/2 tsp. salt	3 c. chopped onions
1 1/2 tsp. pepper	2 1/4 c. peeled chopped
2 tsp. paprika	tomatoes
1 6-lb. rolled roast	1/2 c. sliced mushrooms
1/2 c. cola beverage	1 bay leaf
1/2 c. wine vinegar	1/2 c. sliced stuffed olives
1/4 c. olive oil	

Combine the garlic, salt, pepper and paprika and rub into roast. Place the roast in a bowl. Combine the cola beverage and vinegar and pour over roast. Marinate in refrigerator overnight, turning roast several times. Remove from refrigerator and leave at room temperature for 3 hours. Heat the olive oil in a roasting pan. Drain the roast thoroughly, reserving marinade. Brown roast in olive oil. Place green pepper, onions, tomatoes, mushrooms and bay leaf around roast and pour reserved marinade over the roast. Roast at 300 degrees to desired doneness.

Discard bay leaf and press gravy and the vegetables through a sieve. Add the olives and heat through.

Mrs. Harvey Holland, Aransas Pass, Texas

BEEF SHORT RIBS WITH GRAVY

3 lb. beef short ribs	1 green pepper, cut in 1/2-in.
1 1/2 tsp. salt	squares
1/4 tsp. pepper	4 celery stalks, cut in 1/2-in.
1/4 c. grated onion	diagonal slices
2 lge. carrots, diced	3 tbsp. flour

Brown the short ribs in small amount of fat in a skillet and pour off drippings. Season ribs with salt and pepper and add 1/2 cup water and onion. Cover tightly and cook over low heat for 1 hour and 30 minutes. Add the carrots, green pepper and celery and cook for 30 minutes longer or until beef is tender and vegetables are done. Remove short ribs to a heated platter. Add 2 cups water to the skillet and bring to a boil. Mix the flour with 3 tablespoons water and stir into the carrot mixture. Cook until thickened and serve over short ribs. 6 servings.

Mrs. Henry Sherrer, Bay City, Texas

BAKED STUFFED VEAL

1 lb. boned trimmed veal steak	1 env. seasoned coating mix
6 thin slices cooked ham	for chicken-original flavor
6 thin slices Swiss cheese	

Cut the veal into 6 pieces. Place between 2 pieces of waxed paper and pound to about 1/8-inch thickness. Top each piece of veal with a slice of ham and a slice of cheese. Roll up and secure with wooden pick. Coat with seasoned coating mix according to package directions, then place on an ungreased baking sheet. Bake at 400 degrees for about 20 minutes or until veal is tender. Serve with hot, cooked green peas and pearl onions, if desired. 6 servings.

Baked Stuffed Veal (above)

CREOLE PILAF

1 1/2 c. diced cooked veal	2 stalks celery, chopped
1 c. cooked rice	1 tsp. salt
1 1/2 c. canned tomatoes	1/8 tsp. pepper
1 lge. onion, chopped	Buttered crumbs
1/2 green pepper, chopped	

Mix the veal, rice and tomatoes in a saucepan and cook for 10 minutes. Add the onion, green pepper and celery and season with salt and pepper. Place in a baking dish and cover with buttered crumbs. Bake at 350 degrees for 1 hour. 4 servings.

Mrs. Edna McInnis, Ft. Worth, Texas

FRENCH RISSOLES

2 c. minced cooked veal	1 egg yolk
1 med. onion, minced	1 recipe pastry
Salt and pepper to taste	

Combine all ingredients in a bowl except pastry and blend well. Roll out the pastry on a floured surface, small amount at a time, into 2 1/2-inch circles. Place the veal mixture on half of each circle. Fold over and seal edges. Cook in deep fat at 370 degrees until brown. 1 dozen.

Mrs. L. A. Brown, Oklahoma City, Oklahoma

STUFFED VEAL TIMBALE

2 tbsp. flour	1 sm. package frozen green peas
6 tbsp. cream	1/2 sm. package frozen Brussles sprouts
6 tbsp. carrot juice	1 sm. package frozen green beans
2 eggs, separated	
3/4 lb. ground veal	
Salt and pepper to taste	
2 sm. carrots, sliced	

Mix the flour and cream in a bowl, then stir in the carrot juice and beaten egg yolks. Mix the veal with the seasonings in a bowl and stir in the cream mixture. Beat the egg whites until stiff and fold into the veal mixture. Press most of the veal mixture into a greased 2-quart mold, lining bottom and side and leaving cavity in center. Cook the carrots in boiling, salted water until crisp-tender, then drain. Cook the green peas and Brussles sprouts according to package directions until nearly done, then drain. Place the carrots, peas and Brussles sprouts in cavity of veal mixture. Press remaining veal mixture over top and cover with foil. Place in a pan of hot water. Bake at 350 degrees for about 1 hour, then cool for several minutes. Cook the beans according to package directions and drain. Turn the timbale onto a serving dish and garnish with the beans. Serve with tomato or mushroom sauce, if desired. 4 servings.

Photograph for this recipe on page 44.

LEG OF VEAL

1 4 to 5-lb. leg of veal	1 pt. white wine
1 lb. bacon	3 tbsp. capers
12 anchovies, cut in pieces	1/2 tsp. pepper
Butter	1/2 pt. cream
2 onions, sliced	

Make holes in the veal with a skewer. Cut the bacon in 1-inch long pieces and push a piece of bacon and anchovy into holes. Spread veal with enough butter to seal holes. Melt 1/2 cup butter in a roasting pan and place the leg of veal and onions in the butter. Pour the wine over veal and cover pan. Bake at 300 degrees for about 2 hours or until done. Add the capers and pepper and bake for 15 minutes longer. Place the veal on a serving dish. Pour the pan drippings into a saucepan and add cream. Heat through but do not boil. Serve with veal. May serve with rice if desired. 10 servings.

Mrs. Roland Joyal, Alexandria, Virginia

PIQUANT VEAL ROLLS

1 1/2 lb. thin veal steak	1 egg, beaten
2 tbsp. finely chopped onion	2 c. soft bread crumbs
2 tbsp. butter	2 tbsp. flour
1 tbsp. salt	1 tbsp. fat
1/8 tbsp. pepper	1 c. boiling water

Cut the veal steak into 6 portions. Cook the onion in butter in a saucepan for 1 minute, then stir in the salt, pepper, egg and bread crumbs. Place the onion mixture on the veal portions, fold veal over and fasten with small skewers. Roll in the flour and brown in melted fat in a skillet. Add the water and cover. Cook over low heat for 50 minutes.

Ruby Faye Criswell, Springfield, Arkansas

BROWNED RICE WITH PORK CHOPS

4 pork chops	2/3 c. chopped green pepper
1 c. rice	1/3 c. chopped onion
1 1-lb. can tomatoes	Salt and pepper to taste
1 1/2 c. water	

Brown the pork chops in small amount of fat in a large skillet, then remove from skillet. Place the rice in drippings in the skillet and cook, stirring constantly, until brown. Add the tomatoes, water, green pepper, onion and seasonings and bring to a boil. Place chops over top and cover. Cook over low heat for 30 to 40 minutes or until liquid is absorbed.

Mrs. Ruby H. Bonelli, Vicksburg, Mississippi

Rainbow Pork Chops and Potatoes (below)

RAINBOW PORK CHOPS AND POTATOES

4 lge. loin pork chops	1 1-lb. 1-oz. can fruit cocktail
1/2 tsp. salt	4 sm. sweet potatoes
1/2 tsp. celery salt	1 tbsp. brown sugar
1/4 tsp. marjoram	1/8 tsp. ground allspice

Trim some of the fat from the pork chops and brown in a large heavy frying pan. Add the chops and brown over low heat. Pour off excess fat. Sprinkle the chops with salt, celery salt and marjoram. Drain the syrup from fruit cocktail and pour over the chops. Cover and simmer for about 30 minutes. Pare the potatoes and cut into thick slices. Add to chops and simmer for 30 to 40 minutes or until chops and potatoes are done, turning potatoes 2 or 3 times to absorb gravy. Arrange the chops and potatoes on a large platter and pour most of the pan gravy over top. Add fruit cocktail to frying pan and sprinkle with brown sugar and ground allspice. Cook over high heat, stirring occasionally, until fruit is hot and brown sugar is melted. Spoon over the chops and potatoes and serve at once. 4 servings.

BARBECUED SPARERIBS

3 lb. spareribs	1/4 c. catsup
1 onion, diced	1 tsp. dry mustard
1/4 c. vinegar	1/2 c. water
1 c. tomato juice	1 tbsp. paprika
2 tbsp. brown sugar	1/4 tsp. chili powder
1 tsp. salt	1/8 tsp. cayenne pepper

Cut the spareribs in serving pieces. Cook in a skillet in small amount of fat for about 10 minutes or until brown. Place in a baking pan. Combine remaining ingredients in a saucepan and simmer for about 15 minutes. Pour over spareribs and cover. Bake at 350 degrees for 1 hour and 30 minutes. Remove cover and baste spareribs. Bake for about 15 minutes longer.

Mrs. V. E. Burnett, Okemah, Oklahoma

GLAZED RIBS OF PORK

5 lb. country-style pork ribs	2 tbsp. Dijon mustard
Salt and pepper to taste	Cooked prunes
1 jar currant jelly	Salad greens
2 tbsp. prepared mustard	

Remove most of the fat from the ribs, then season ribs with salt and pepper. Place in a roasting pan, rib side down. Roast at 350 degrees for about 1 hour and 30 minutes, basting occasionally with pan drippings. Melt the jelly in a saucepan. Add the mustards and mix well. Increase oven temperature to 425 degrees. Baste the ribs with the jelly mixture and bake for about 10 minutes longer or until glazed. Cut the ribs into serving pieces and place on a platter. Garnish with cooked prunes and greens. 6-8 servings.

Photograph for this recipe on cover.

PORK TENDERLOIN WITH SWEET POTATOES AND APPLES

1 pork tenderloin	4 tsp. sugar
1 c. milk	4 tsp. seedless raisins
1/2 c. seasoned flour	Cinnamon to taste
2 tbsp. fat	4 peeled apples, cored
4 peeled sweet potatoes, quartered	4 marshmallows

Dip the pork in milk and dredge with seasoned flour. Brown in fat in a Dutch oven and place sweet potatoes around pork. Mix the sugar, raisins and cinnamon and place in center of apples. Place apples around pork. Add remaining milk and cover. Cook over low heat for 1 hour and 15 minutes or until tenderloin is done. Place a marshmallow on top of each apple and cook until marshmallows are melted.

Mrs. Herman A. Wolff, King, North Carolina

FRIED SALT PORK WITH CREAM GRAVY

1/2 lb. fat salt pork	1 1/2 c. milk
2 tbsp. flour	Pepper to taste

Wash and dice the salt pork. Fry in a skillet over low heat until crisp, then place in a serving dish. Pour off all the fat from skillet except 2 tablespoons. Add the flour to remaining fat and blend. Stir in the milk gradually and bring to a boil, stirring constantly. Reduce heat and simmer for 5 minutes. Season with pepper and pour over the salt pork. Sausage patties may be substituted for the salt pork.

Mrs. Frank Stewart, Raleigh, North Carolina

Fruit-Crowned Ham Loaf (below)

FRUIT-CROWNED HAM LOAF

1 lb. ground ham	1 1-lb. 1-oz. can fruit
1 lb. ground pork	cocktail
2 eggs, beaten	1/2 lemon, sliced
1 c. rye cracker crumbs	1 3-in. cinnamon stick
1/4 c. finely chopped green	2 whole cloves
pepper	1 1/2 tsp. cornstarch
1 tbsp. instant minced onion	Parsley

Combine the ham, pork, eggs, crumbs, green pepper and onion in a bowl and mix well. Place a custard cup in bottom of a medium mixing bowl and press ham mixture into bowl over cup. Invert on a shallow baking pan and remove bowl and custard cup. Bake in a 350-degree oven for 1 hour. Drain the fruit cocktail, reserving syrup. Add enough water to reserved syrup to make 1 cup liquid and place in a saucepan. Add the lemon slices, cinnamon stick and cloves and simmer for 10 minutes. Remove cinnamon stick and cloves. Blend the cornstarch with small amount of cold water, then stir into the syrup. Cook and stir until clear and thickened. Add fruit cocktail and heat through. Spoon fat out of well made by custard cup and place loaf on a serving plate. Garnish with parsley and fill well with fruit sauce. Other crackers may be substituted for rye crackers, if desired. 8 servings.

CREOLE PORK SAUSAGE

4 lb. lean fresh pork	2 lge. onions, minced
2 lb. fat fresh pork	1 clove of garlic, minced
3 tsp. salt	1 sprig of thyme, minced
2 tsp. pepper	1 sprig of parsley, minced
1/2 tsp. cayenne pepper	2 bay leaves, crushed
1/2 tsp. chili pepper	1/2 tsp. allspice
1 tsp. paprika	Cleaned casings

Grind the lean and fat pork fine and place in a large container. Add the seasonings and mix thoroughly. Add remaining ingredients except the casings and mix well. Scald the casings. Wash and dry. Fill with sausage mixture and tie in lengths. 6 pounds.

Mrs. Alvin A. Coombs, Columbia, South Carolina

BAKED HAM WITH BRANDY SAUCE

1 12 to 14-lb. country-cured ham	Honey
Cloves	6 c. apple cider
Brown sugar	1 c. orange juice
	1/4 c. brandy

Place the ham in a large metal container and cover with water. Soak ham overnight, then drain. Cover with fresh water and bring to a boil. Reduce heat and simmer for about 2 hours and 30 minutes or until the ham is tender. Drain the ham. Remove rind and some of the fat. Score the fat on the ham in diamond shapes and stud with cloves. Place in a roaster and cover with brown sugar and honey. Pour 2 cups apple cider into the roaster. Bake at 450 degrees until brown, basting frequently with liquid in roaster. Place the ham on a platter and slice. Mix remaining apple cider, 1 pound brown sugar, 6 cloves and the orange juice in a saucepan and bring to a boil. Add the brandy and remove from heat. Remove the cloves and serve with the ham. Apple juice may be substituted for apple cider.

Mrs. Dot Carney, Richmond, Virginia

CREOLE LAMB CHOPS

4 lamb chops	1/2 c. diced onions
Seasoned flour	1/2 c. tomato soup
2 tbsp. shortening	1/2 c. water

Trim the lamb chops and dip in seasoned flour. Cook in a skillet in shortening until light brown. Sprinkle with onions. Mix the soup and water and pour over the chops. Cover. Bake in 325-degree oven for 1 hour and 30 minutes or until chops are tender.

Paulette Hairston, Section, Alabama

LAMB CHOPS WITH MADEIRA

2 tbsp. butter	1/8 tsp. pepper
3 onions, minced	1/2 tsp. salt
2 carrots, minced	6 lamb chops
4 mushrooms, minced	1 tsp. tomato paste
1/2 clove of garlic, minced	2 tbsp. Madeira

Melt the butter in a skillet. Add the onions, carrots, mushrooms and garlic and cover. Cook over low heat until tender. Season with pepper and salt. Place the lamb chops on a broiler pan and broil until brown. Place on a platter. Add tomato paste and Madeira to vegetable mixture and serve on lamb chops.

Mrs. V. W. Hobson, Baton Rouge, Louisiana

Shoulder Lamb Chops with Okra (below)

SHOULDER LAMB CHOPS WITH OKRA

1/3 c. chopped onion	1/4 tsp. coarsely ground pepper
2 tbsp. salad oil	1/4 tsp. rubbed sage
4 shoulder lamb chops,	1/4 tsp. basil
1 in. thick	1/4 tsp. thyme leaves
1 1-lb. can tomatoes	1 slice lemon peel
2 tbsp. tomato paste	1 10-oz. package frozen
1 tsp. salt	whole baby okra

Saute the onion in oil in a large skillet until tender, then remove from skillet. Saute the lamb chops in the skillet until browned on both sides. Drain off excess drippings. Mix the tomatoes, tomato paste, seasonings, lemon peel and onion and add to chops in the skillet. Bring to a boil and cover. Reduce heat and simmer for 30 to 35 minutes or until chops are nearly tender. Add the frozen okra, separating pieces with a fork, and cook for 10 minutes longer. Remove the lemon peel. 4 servings.

LAMB AND EGGPLANT

3 med. eggplant, cut in	6 fresh tomatoes
1/4-in. slices	Salt and pepper to taste
1/4 c. olive oil	3 c. chopped cooked lamb
3 onions, thinly sliced	2 eggs, well beaten
6 lge. mushrooms, sliced	1/2 c. heavy cream
4 tbsp. butter	1/2 c. minced parsley

Soak the eggplant in salted water to cover for 1 hour, then drain well. Saute in olive oil in a skillet until brown. Saute the onions and mushrooms in 2 table-spoons butter in a saucepan until golden brown. Peel and chop the tomatoes and saute in remaining butter until tender. Add salt and pepper. Place alternate layers of eggplant, lamb, mushroom mixture and tomatoes in a large casserole.

Bake at 350 degrees for 45 minutes or until eggplant is tender. Mix the eggs and cream and pour over casserole. Sprinkle with parsley and bake until set. 10 servings.

Mrs. Harold J. Heckel, Fayetteville, Arkansas

LAMB BARBECUE

1 sm. onion, sliced	1/4 c. water
1 tbsp. butter or margarine	1 tsp. Worcestershire sauce
2 tbsp. vinegar	1 c. cubed cooked lamb
2 tsp. brown sugar	Buttered noodles
1/2 c. catsup	

Saute the onion in butter in a blazer pan until tender. Add the vinegar, brown sugar, catsup, water and Worcestershire sauce and cover. Simmer for 15 minutes. Add the lamb and cook until heated through. Place blazer pan over water pan and keep hot. Serve lamb mixture over noodles. 2 servings.

Edna Mae Basden, Rienzi, Mississippi

HERBED ROAST LEG OF LAMB

1 garlic clove, crushed	1 tsp. thyme
1 tsp. salt	1 tsp. rosemary
Pepper to taste	2 tbsp. flour
2 tbsp. olive oil	1 c. dry white wine
1 6-lb. leg of lamb	1 c. water
1 tsp. marjoram	

Combine the garlic with salt and pepper and mix with the olive oil. Rub on the leg of lamb and sprinkle lamb with marjoram, thyme, rosemary and flour. Place the lamb in a roasting pan and pour the wine and water into pan. Roast at 325 degrees for 2 hours and 30 minutes, basting frequently.

Mrs. E. F. Bonvicin, Holloman Air Force Base, New Mexico

STUFFED SHOULDER OF LAMB

1 4-lb. shoulder of lamb	1 1/2 c. chopped tomatoes
2 bay leaves, crushed	1 tsp. salt
1 onion, finely chopped	1 c. cooked rice
1 green pepper, finely chopped	

Have shoulder of lamb boned to make a pocket for stuffing. Melt small amount of fat in a skillet. Add the bay leaves, onion and green pepper and cook until tender. Add the tomatoes and salt and cook for 5 minutes. Stir in the rice and fill pocket of lamb. Fasten with skewers or tie with string. Place on a rack in a baking pan, fat side up. Bake in 325-degree oven for about 2 hours and 30 minutes or until done.

Mrs. William Taylor, Wilmington, Delaware

EXCITING LAMB CASSEROLE

3 onions, sliced	1 tbsp. soy sauce
1 green onion, sliced	1 beef bouillon cube
1 Winesap apple, cut in strips	2 lb. lamb
1 green pepper, cut in strips	1 tsp. curry
2 tbsp. margarine	Salt to taste
1 tbsp. chutney	Flour

Cook the onions, green onion, apple and green pepper in the margarine in a large skillet until tender but not brown. Add 1 cup water, chutney, soy sauce and bouillon cube and cover. Simmer for about 15 minutes. Cut the lamb into bite-sized pieces and sprinkle with curry and salt. Coat with flour and fry in a skillet in small amount of fat until brown. Add to the onion mixture and simmer for 15 minutes longer, adding water, if needed. Serve with rice and additional chutney.

Photograph for this recipe on page 2.

CHITTERLINGS

2 lb. chitterlings	1 egg, slightly beaten
1 tbsp. whole cloves	1 tbsp. water
1 red pepper, chopped	Cracker crumbs

Wash the chitterlings thoroughly and place in a saucepan. Cover with boiling salted water. Add the cloves and red pepper and cook until tender. Drain. Cut in 2-inch pieces. Mix the egg with water. Dip the chitterlings into the egg mixture, then coat with cracker crumbs. Fry in deep fat at 370 degrees until brown. 4-6 servings.

Mrs. Thomas Billingsley, Louisville, Kentucky

KIDNEY A LA FRANCAISE

1 beef kidney	1/2 tsp. salt
Flour	1/8 tsp. pepper
2 tbsp. shortening	1 lemon slice
1 bay leaf	

Soak the kidney in cold water in a saucepan for 1 hour, changing water 2 or 3 times. Cover with cold water and bring to boiling point. Drain. Cover with cold water and bring to boiling point. Drain, then cover with cold water. Bring to boiling point and reduce heat. Simmer for 10 minutes. Remove from heat and cool. Drain. Cut out the cords and most of the center fat and slice thin. Dip in flour. Saute in shortening in a skillet until brown. Remove from skillet. Add 1/4 cup flour to skillet drippings and cook, stirring, until well browned. Add 1 1/2 cups boiling water and cook, stirring, until smooth. Return kidney slices to skillet and add bay leaf, salt, pepper and lemon slice. Cover. Simmer for 1 hour, adding water, if necessary. Remove bay leaf.

Mrs. M. N. Jones, Memphis, Tennessee

SPAGHETTINI WITH HOT SAUSAGE SAUCE

1 lb. Italian hot sausage
1/4 c. hot water
1/2 lb. medium mushrooms,
  sliced
3/4 c. shredded carrots
1 med. onion, sliced
1/2 c. chopped celery
1/4 c. chopped parsley
2 lb. ground beef chuck
1 1-lb. 12-oz. can plum tomatoes

2 6-oz. cans tomato paste
1 c. dry red wine
1 bay leaf
Salt
1 tsp. basil leaves
1/4 tsp. pepper (opt.)
6 to 9 qt. boiling water
1 1/2 lb. spaghettini or
  spaghetti
Grated Parmesan cheese (opt.)

Cut the sausage into chunks and place in a Dutch oven or kettle. Add the hot water and cover tightly. Cook for 10 minutes, stirring occasionally. Remove sausage with slotted spoon. Saute the mushrooms, carrots, onion, celery and parsley in sausage drippings in the Dutch oven until crisp-tender, then remove from Dutch oven. Place the ground chuck in the Dutch oven and cook, stirring frequently, until lightly browned and all liquid is evaporated. Remove any excess fat. Return sausage and vegetables to the Dutch oven. Add the tomatoes, tomato paste, wine, bay leaf, 2 teaspoons salt, basil and pepper. Cover and simmer for 30 minutes. Uncover and simmer for 1 hour and 30 minutes, stirring occasionally. Add 3 tablespoons salt to boiling water and add spaghettini gradually so that water continues to boil. Cook, stirring occasionally, until tender, then drain in a colander. Serve with sausage sauce and Parmesan cheese. 12 servings.

Spaghettini with Hot Sausage Sauce (above)

BAKED LIVER

1 1 1/2-lb. liver	2 tbsp. bacon drippings
2 tsp. salt	2 med. onions, thinly sliced
1/2 tsp. pepper	2 1/2 c. canned tomatoes
Flour	

Season the liver with salt and pepper and dredge with flour. Brown in drippings in a skillet and place in a Dutch oven. Add the onions. Pour tomatoes into the skillet in which the liver was browned and stir to loosen browned particles. Pour over the liver and cover. Bake at 350 degrees for 1 hour and 30 minutes. 6-8 servings.

Mrs. Sallie Shultz, Cromwell, Kentucky

FRIED LIVER AND ONIONS

1 lb. sliced liver	1 tsp. pepper
1 c. flour	1/2 c. shortening
1 tsp. salt	1 onion, sliced

Dredge the liver with flour and season with salt and pepper. Heat the shortening in a skillet. Add the liver and cook over low heat until brown. Add the onion and cook until tender.

Mrs. G. C. Booker, Theodore, Alabama

SPANISH SWEETBREADS

2 lb. sweetbreads	1 sm. onion, chopped
Salt and pepper to taste	1 jalapeno pepper, chopped
Flour	1/2 c. water
1 No. 303 can tomatoes	

Slice the sweetbreads and season with salt and pepper. Roll in flour and brown in small amount of fat in a skillet. Add the tomatoes, onion, jalapeno pepper and water and bring to a boil. Reduce heat and simmer for 20 minutes.

Mrs. Brenda Shiver, Miami, Florida

LAMB AND SAUSAGE

5 lamb shoulder chops	1/4 lb. mushrooms
1 tsp. bacon fat	2 tbsp. butter
5 pineapple slices, drained	3 tomatoes, peeled and halved
5 med. sweet potatoes	Salt and pepper to taste
5 pork sausages	3/4 c. pineapple juice

Brown the lamb chops in fat and place in a shallow casserole. Place 1 slice pineapple over each chop. Peel the potatoes and slice 1/2 inch thick. Arrange around chops and add sausages. Saute the mushrooms in butter in a saucepan until tender and place in casserole. Add the tomatoes, salt and pepper. Add the pineapple juice and cover casserole. Bake at 350 degrees for 45 minutes or until tender. 5 servings.

Mrs. John C. Martin, Fort Hood, Texas

CREOLE TRIPE

1 lb. honeycomb tripe	**1 bay leaf**
2 tbsp. fat	**1/4 tsp. powdered thyme**
2 tbsp. flour	**1/2 hot pepper, chopped**
3/4 c. chopped onions	**2 c. water**
1/2 c. chopped green pepper	**Salt and pepper to taste**
1 No. 2 can tomatoes	

Wash the tripe and place in a kettle. Cover with water and bring to a boil. Reduce heat and simmer for 20 minutes. Drain and cut into small pieces. Place the fat in a deep frying pan and brown the flour in the fat. Add the onions and green pepper and cook until tender. Add the tomatoes and cook for 5 minutes. Add bay leaf, thyme, hot pepper, water, salt, pepper and tripe and pour into a casserole. Bake at 350 degrees for 1 hour, adding water if needed. 6 servings.

Mrs. Maurice George, Bay St. Louis, Mississippi

HAM JAMBALAYA

1 med. onion, chopped	**1 tsp. salt**
1 clove of garlic, mashed	**1 tsp. pepper**
1 green pepper, chopped	**4 c. boiling water**
2 tbsp. salad oil	**2 c. diced cooked ham**
1 tbsp. flour	**1/2 lb. cleaned cooked shrimp**
1 c. canned tomatoes	**1 c. rice**
1/2 tsp. thyme	**Dash of hot sauce**
1/2 bay leaf, crushed	**1 tsp. Worcestershire sauce**

Cook the onion, garlic and green pepper in oil in a large saucepan until tender but not browned. Stir in the flour and cook until smooth. Add the tomatoes, thyme, bay leaf, salt, pepper and water and simmer for 10 minutes. Add the ham and shrimp. Bring to a boil and stir in the rice, hot sauce and Worcestershire sauce. Cook for about 20 minutes, stirring occasionally. 6 servings.

Mrs. J. R. Hightower, Itta Bena, Mississippi

VEAL AND HAM PIE

1 6-oz. can sliced mushrooms	**1 c. diced cooked ham**
2 c. medium white sauce	**2 c. cooked green beans or peas**
1/4 tsp. nutmeg	**6 unbaked biscuits**
2 c. diced cooked veal	

Saute the mushrooms in small amount of fat in a saucepan until lightly browned. Mix with white sauce, nutmeg, veal, ham and beans. Pour into a greased 2-quart casserole and top with biscuits. Bake at 350 degrees for 25 minutes. Diluted mushroom soup may be substituted for white sauce. 6 servings.

Mrs. Robert E. Pollock, Maysville, North Carolina

Nectarine-Glazed Duckling (page 68)

creole fowl and game

When a Creole cook described an animal as a "fowl," she meant not only domestic turkey and chicken but also the duck, dove, goose, pheasant, squab, quail, and wild turkey so abundant in the forests and waters around her home. These fowl, together with such game animals as rabbit, squirrel, and deer, were an important part of the Creole family's diet. Wise household economy required that when such abundance was available, it be used to feed the family.

Thus generations of Creole women developed subtly flavored recipes that featured fowl and game in many dishes. Some of the most prized of these recipes have been gathered here in hopes that your family will enjoy them as they have been enjoyed in the South for years.

When you are looking for an unusual main dish, why not feature Fried Rabbit or Squirrel Pie. Both have been favorites with Creole families – and are certain to become popular with your family, too. And if deer hunting is a sport your family enjoys, then you'll delight in being able to serve them Venison Steaks, delicious meat with its flavor highlighted by seasonings as only the Creoles use them.

Depend on the recipes you'll discover in this section to lead you and your family into a brand-new adventure in fine eating, an adventure that will make you think you are dining in the finest Creole homes!

FRIED RABBIT

1 rabbit or squirrel	**2 slices bacon**
Seasoned flour	

Cut the rabbit into serving pieces and dip into seasoned flour. Fry the bacon in a frying pan until crisp and remove from frying pan. Add the rabbit to bacon grease and cook until brown. Reduce heat and add small amount of hot water. Cover and cook until rabbit is tender.

Mrs. Lula S. Patrick, Monticello, Kentucky

RABBIT RAGOUT

3 rabbits	**1 c. chopped onions**
3 qt. water	**4 c. cooked tomatoes, drained**
1/4 c. diced bacon	**2 c. diced potatoes**
1/4 tsp. cayenne pepper	**2 c. lima beans**
2 tsp. salt	**2 c. corn**
1/4 tsp. pepper	

Cut the rabbits in serving pieces and place in a large kettle. Add the water and bring to a boil. Reduce heat and simmer until rabbits are tender, skimming surface occasionally. Remove rabbits from liquid and cool. Remove rabbit from bones and return to liquid. Add remaining ingredients except corn and cook for 1 hour. Add the corn and cook for 10 minutes longer. 6-8 servings.

Mrs. Cam B. Comer, Sr., Peachland, North Carolina

SQUIRREL WITH RICE

2 slices salt pork, diced	**1/4 c. catsup**
2 squirrels, disjointed	**1/2 onion, sliced**
2 qt. water	**Salt and pepper to taste**
1 c. rice	

Cook the salt pork in a large saucepan until partially done. Add the squirrels and cook until brown. Add the water and simmer until squirrels are tender, adding water as needed. Add the rice, catsup, onion and seasonings and cook until rice is tender, adding water as needed.

Mrs. Jack Adams, Miami, Oklahoma

SQUIRREL PIE

3 squirrels	**1 10-oz. package frozen peas**
5 med. potatoes, chopped	**1 10-oz. package frozen corn**
4 carrots, chopped	**1 recipe for 2-crust pie**
1 lge. onion, chopped	

Cook the squirrels in boiling, salted water for about 2 hours or until tender. Drain and reserve broth. Cool the squirrels and remove squirrel bones. Cook the potatoes, carrots and onion in boiling reserved broth until tender, then drain. Cook the peas and corn according to package directions and drain. Combine squirrel and vegetables and place in bottom crust in a pie pan. Apply top crust and seal edges. Cut slits in top crust. Bake in 400-degree oven for 40 minutes or until brown.

Mrs. Dan Conrad, Charleston, West Virginia

MARENGO CASSEROLE

3 lb. venison	Margarine or butter
1 bottle dry white wine	1 can consomme
7 or 8 white peppercorns	1 can tomato sauce
7 or 8 black peppercorns	3 to 4 tbsp. flour
4 bay leaves	Salt and pepper to taste
1/2 lb. sliced salt pork	1 tbsp. dry sherry (opt.)
1 lb. small onions	1 tbsp. brandy (opt.)
1 lb. fresh mushrooms	

Place the venison in a shallow pan. Mix the wine, peppercorns and bay leaves and pour over the venison. Refrigerate for 2 to 3 days, turning venison occasionally. Drain the venison, then strain and reserve the marinade. Wipe the venison dry and place on a rack in a roasting pan. Wash the salt pork and place over venison. Pour 1 1/2 cups water into the pan and add about 1 cup reserved marinade. Bake at 325 degrees for about 2 hours or until done, basting with pan drippings occasionally. Peel the onions and cook in boiling, salted water until tender. Cook the mushrooms in small amount of margarine until lightly browned. Cut the venison into bite-sized pieces and place in a large frypan. Add the onions, mushrooms, consomme, tomato sauce and 1 cup pan drippings. Mix the flour with 1/4 cup water until smooth and stir into the venison mixture. Add the salt, pepper, sherry and brandy and simmer for about 15 minutes or until thickened, stirring frequently. Serve with boiled potatoes and green beans. May be prepared the day before serving and reheated.

VENISON STEAK

2 tbsp. flour	4 tbsp. shortening
1 1/2 to 2 lb. venison round steak	1 c. water
	1 onion, sliced
Salt and pepper to taste	1/2 c. chopped celery

Pound the flour into steak with meat hammer or saucer edge and sprinkle with salt and pepper. Heat the shortening in heavy skillet. Add the steak and brown on both sides. Add the water, onion and celery and cover. Simmer for about 1 hour and 30 minutes, adding water, if necessary. Remove steak and place on a platter. Thicken liquid with additional flour mixed with water. 4-6 servings.

Mrs. Joseph Coss, Wellsburg, West Virginia

BAKED DOVE

30 dove breasts	3 cloves of garlic, crushed
1/4 c. steak sauce	(opt.)
2 c. red wine	Salt and pepper to taste
1/4 c. oil	4 slices bacon, diced
1/4 c. Worcestershire sauce	Paprika to taste

Place the dove breasts, skin side down, in a shallow baking pan. Combine remaining ingredients except bacon and paprika and pour over dove breasts. Marinate for 15 to 20 minutes. Sprinkle the bacon and paprika over dove breasts. Bake in 425-degree oven for 20 minutes. Reduce temperature to 350 degrees and bake for 30 minutes or until tender.

Mrs. Norman C. Germroth, Phoenix, Arizona

DOVE WITH WINE SAUCE

8 dove breasts	1 1/4 c. sherry
Salt to taste	1 can beef gravy
Seasoned flour	1/2 c. honey
Bacon drippings	Juice of 1/2 lemon
3/4 c. water	2 tsp. Worcestershire sauce

Season the dove breasts with salt and let stand for about 15 minutes. Shake in a bag with seasoned flour. Brown in bacon drippings in a skillet. Place in a pressure cooker with water and 1/4 cup sherry and cook at 15 pounds pressure for about 10 minutes. Run water over pressure cooker to return pressure to normal, then place dove in a baking dish. Combine remaining sherry and remaining ingredients and pour over the dove breasts. Bake at 350 degrees for 2 hours. 4 servings.

Mrs. E. E. Hough, Treasure Island, Florida

NECTARINE-GLAZED DUCKLING

1 4 1/2 to 5-lb. duckling	2 or 3 peeled onions
1/2 tsp. salt	2 or 3 fresh nectarines
1/4 tsp. garlic salt	1/2 c. red currant jelly
1/4 tsp. pepper	

Rub the duckling skin and cavity with the salt, garlic salt and pepper. Stuff with onions and truss. Place, breast side up, on a rack in a roasting pan. Roast at 325 degrees for 2 hours and 30 minutes to 3 hours or until thick portion of leg feels tender, draining fat from pan twice. Cut into quarters with shears. Chop enough nectarines fine to make 1 cup fruit and juice. Combine with the jelly in a saucepan and heat until jelly is melted. Spoon over duckling twice during last 30 minutes of roasting, using 1/4 cup each time. Chop about 1/2 cup nectarines and stir into remaining glaze. Heat through and serve with the duckling. Two or 3 small unpared apples may be substituted for the onions. 4 servings.

Photograph for this recipe on page 64.

ROAST DUCK WITH ORANGE GRAVY

2   4 1/2 to 5-lb. ready-to-
   cook ducklings with giblets
Salt
1 c. freshly squeezed orange
   juice
1/2 onion, sliced
1 bay leaf
Dash of pepper

2 California oranges, peeled
3 tbsp. brown sugar
1/3 c. flour
1 tsp. freshly grated orange
   peel
2 tsp. Worcestershire sauce
1 tsp. bottled browning sauce

Preheat oven to 450 degrees. Rinse the ducks. Drain thoroughly and wipe dry inside and out with paper towels. Rub cavities with salt. Remove fat from neck opening and secure skin to back with skewer, cutting away extra skin. Tie legs together, leaving 3 inches between, and pierce entire surface of ducks with fork. Place, breast side up, on a rack in a shallow roasting pan. Place in oven and turn temperature down to 325 degrees immediately. Bake for about 2 hours and 30 minutes or until done, basting with orange juice during the last 1 hour and 30 minutes of baking. Place the giblets, 2 3/4 cups water, onion, bay leaf, 1 teaspoon salt and pepper in a saucepan and cover. Simmer for about 1 hour and 30 minutes, adding water as needed. Strain the broth. Cut the oranges into bite-sized pieces and place in a bowl. Sprinkle with 2 tablespoons brown sugar. Remove ducks from pan, draining juice from cavities into pan, and keep warm on a serving platter. Skim most of the fat from pan carefully, reserving 1 cup bottom drippings. Blend reserved drippings with flour in a saucepan until smooth. Stir in the giblet broth slowly. Add 1/4 teaspoon salt, orange peel, remaining brown sugar and sauces. Bring to a boil over medium heat, stirring constantly, and boil for 2 to 3 minutes. Stir in orange pieces and serve with ducks. 6-8 servings.

Roast Duck with Orange Gravy (above)

DUCK A L'ORANGE

1 5 to 6-lb. duck	1 c. orange marmalade
2 tbsp. butter	Salt and pepper to taste
Flour	1 onion, peeled
Kitchen Bouquet	3 oranges, peeled

Remove giblets and neck from cavity of duck and place in a saucepan. Cover with salted water and bring to a boil. Reduce heat and simmer for 45 minutes. Remove neck and giblets from stock and discard neck. Chop giblets. Cook stock until reduced to 1 cup, if necessary. Melt butter in a saucepan and blend in 2 tablespoons flour until smooth. Add the stock and cook, stirring constantly, until thickened. Add giblets and enough Kitchen Bouquet to make gravy a dark color. Add the marmalade and mix well. Set aside. Season duck inside and out with salt and pepper. Place onion and 1 orange inside duck and close cavity. Place duck on rack in roasting pan. Bake at 450 degrees for 30 minutes. Reduce temperature to 350 degrees and pour gravy over duck. Bake for 1 hour longer, basting occasionally. Remove duck from pan and place on a platter. Section remaining oranges and place around duck. Drain excess fat from roasting pan and thicken pan drippings with flour mixed with water. Serve with duck. 5 servings.

Mrs. Gwinn Matthews, Ripley, Tennessee

WILD DUCK CREOLE

2 wild ducks	4 sm. onions
Salt to taste	4 carrots
2 lge. onions	3 sprigs of parsley, chopped
1 tbsp. flour	2 c. tomato juice
2 tbsp. melted butter or	Juice of 1 orange
margarine	2 c. consomme
2 slices bacon	Pepper to taste

Rub ducks inside and out with salt and place in a baking dish. Place 1 large onion inside each duck. Mix the flour with butter and rub over breasts of ducks. Place 1 slice bacon on each duck. Bake in 450-degree oven for 15 minutes. Add small onions, carrots and parsley. Combine the tomato juice, orange juice and consomme in a saucepan and bring to a boil. Add salt and pepper and pour over ducks. Cover. Reduce temperature to 350 degrees and bake until ducks are tender. 4 servings.

Mrs. T. J. Zeman, Memphis, Tennessee

BRAISED WILD GOOSE

1 wild goose	2 bay leaves
Salt pork or bacon slices	1 tsp. thyme
1 onion, sliced	1 qt. consomme
1 lge. carrot, sliced	1 tbsp. cornstarch
1 stalk celery, chopped	2 tbsp. water

Clean the goose thoroughly and remove any shot. Place in a baking pan and cover with salt pork. Bake at 400 degrees until well browned. Remove from oven and pour off fat from pan. Add remaining ingredients except cornstarch and water to pan and cover. Reduce temperature to 325 degrees and bake for 2 hours and 30 minutes to 3 hours and 30 minutes or until tender, basting frequently. Remove goose from bones and place in a deep serving dish. Strain the gravy and thicken with mixture of cornstarch and water. Pour over goose. Serve with wild rice, if desired.

Mrs. F. R. Kadie, Poolesville, Maryland

CRANBERRY-BAKED CORNISH HENS

3 c. fresh cranberries	1/4 c. butter or margarine
1 c. water	2 tsp. grated orange rind
1/4 c. frozen concentrated orange juice	Pinch of poultry seasoning
	6 Cornish hens
1 1/2 c. sugar	Salt and pepper to taste

Combine the cranberries, water and orange juice concentrate in a saucepan and cook over medium heat until cranberries begin to pop. Remove from heat and stir in the sugar, butter, orange rind and poultry seasoning. Sprinkle hens inside and out with salt and pepper. Truss and place on a rack in a shallow roasting pan. Roast according to package directions, brushing liberally with cranberry mixture every 5 minutes during last 30 minutes of roasting.

Cranberry-Baked Cornish Hens (above)

GUINEA HENS WITH ORANGE SAUCE

2 guinea hens	1 bouillon cube
Salt and pepper to taste	1/2 c. hot water
4 tbsp. butter	1/2 c. white wine or dry
1 tbsp. grated orange rind	vermouth
2 peeled oranges, quartered	

Cut the guinea hens in serving pieces and season with salt and pepper. Brown in butter in a skillet. Add the orange rind and oranges. Dissolve bouillon cube in hot water and stir into orange mixture. Stir in the wine and cover. Bake at 300 degrees for 2 hours. Serve the guinea hens with sauce over rice or wild rice. 4-6 servings.

Mrs. Fred Moore, Baton Rouge, Louisiana

BROILED PARTRIDGE

3 young partridge	Juice of 1 lemon
Salt and pepper to taste	1 glass wine
Melted butter	Chopped parsley to taste
6 slices toast	

Rub each partridge with salt and pepper and 2 tablespoons melted butter. Split down back and place in broiler pan, skin side up. Broil for 25 to 30 minutes or until done, turning frequently. Dip slices of toast in lemon juice and wine. Brush butter on toast and sprinkle with salt and pepper. Place partridge on toast and pour melted butter and small amount of drippings over partridge. Sprinkle with parsley. 3 servings.

Mrs. Ray Rhymes, Macon, Mississippi

ROASTED PHEASANT

1 pheasant	1 c. wild rice
Salt and pepper to taste	1 c. apricot juice

Place the pheasant on a large piece of aluminum foil, then place in a roaster. Rub cavity with salt and pepper and place the rice in cavity. Pour the apricot juice over pheasant and wrap tightly with foil. Bake at 325 degrees for 1 hour or until pheasant is tender. Other juices may be substituted for apricot juice. 4 servings.

Mrs. Al Davis, Dothan, Alabama

PHEASANT JAMBALAYA

2 pheasant	1/4 tsp. thyme
1/2 lb. ham, cut in cubes	1/4 tsp. hot sauce
3 tbsp. vegetable oil	1/4 tsp. pepper
1 c. chopped green pepper	Salt to taste
1 lge. onion, chopped	3 c. hot water
1 clove of garlic, minced	1 1/2 c. rice
2 tsp. Worcestershire sauce	

Cut the pheasant in serving pieces. Brown the pheasant and ham in oil in a skillet, then remove from skillet. Saute the green pepper, onion and garlic in same skillet for 5 minutes over low heat. Add the seasonings and water and simmer for 10 minutes. Add the rice and meats and cover. Cook over low heat for 25 minutes. Fluff rice with a fork and cook for 5 minutes longer. 8 servings.

Mrs. Tom Bowden, San Antonio, Texas

BAKED QUAIL

Quail	**1/4 tsp. pepper**
1/2 c. sherry or white wine	**1/4 tsp. thyme**
1 sm. onion, minced	**1/2 c. margarine**
1/2 tsp. salt	

Fry the quail in small amount of fat in a skillet until brown, then place in a baking pan. Combine remaining ingredients in a saucepan and bring to a boil. Pour over quail and cover with foil. Bake at 350 degrees for 45 minutes to 1 hour or until tender. Serve with rice or wild rice.

Mrs. William H. Foushee, Sr., Southern Pines, North Carolina

SOUTHERN-FRIED QUAIL

Quail	**Flour**
Salt and pepper to taste	

Season the quail with salt and pepper and dredge with flour. Place in deep frying pan half filled with hot fat. Cook for several minutes over high heat, then cover. Reduce heat and cook until tender, turning to brown. Serve on a hot platter and garnish with lemon slices and parsley sprigs.

Mrs. Mae B. Plemmons, Chester, South Carolina

SQUAB CASSEROLE

6 squab	**1 c. chicken stock**
Salt and pepper	**1 tbsp. butter**
1 sprig of parsley	**1 tbsp. flour**
1 sm. carrot, diced	**12 mushrooms, sauteed**
1 sm. onion, diced	**1 tbsp. catsup**
1 bay leaf	**2 tbsp. sherry**

Season the squab with salt and pepper and place in a casserole. Add the parsley, carrot, onion, bay leaf and chicken stock and cover. Bake at 350 degrees for about 1 hour or until squab are tender. Drain squab and reserve liquid. Melt the butter in a saucepan and blend in flour. Add reserved liquid and cook until thickened, stirring constantly. Add mushrooms, catsup and sherry and pour over squab. Bake until heated through. 6 servings.

Mrs. R. K. Jeffries, Alexandria, Louisiana

Spitted Squab with Brussels Sprouts (below)

SPITTED SQUAB WITH BRUSSELS SPROUTS

1 sm. onion, sliced	6 squab
1/3 c. butter or margarine	Salt
3/4 c. sauterne	Pepper to taste
1/4 tsp. tarragon leaves	1/4 c. water
Dash of cayenne pepper	2 10-oz. packages frozen
2 tsp. Worcestershire sauce	California Brussels sprouts
2 tsp. lemon juice	Toasted buttered bread crumbs

Saute the onion in butter in a medium saucepan until crisp-tender. Add the sauterne, tarragon, cayenne pepper, Worcestershire sauce and lemon juice and simmer for 5 minutes. Sprinkle the squab inside and out with salt to taste and pepper and truss. Place on spit and cook in rotisserie at 375 degrees for 40 minutes, basting frequently with the butter mixture. Add the water and 1/4 teaspoon salt to remaining butter mixture and bring to a boil. Add the Brussels sprouts and cover. Cook for about 15 minutes or until Brussels sprouts are just tender. Drain and reserve the liquid. Serve squab and Brussels sprouts on bed of bread crumbs with reserved liquid. 6 servings.

SQUAB PILAU

6 slices bacon, diced	4 eggs, beaten
3/4 c. chopped celery	Salt and pepper to taste
1 onion, chopped	4 squab, dressed
2 c. rice	Pickle juice
4 c. chicken stock	

Fry the bacon in a skillet until crisp and remove from skillet. Brown the celery and onion in bacon drippings. Cook the rice in chicken stock until tender, then add the bacon, celery and onion. Stir in the eggs and season with salt and pepper. Stuff the squab with rice mixture and place on mounds of remaining rice mixture in a baking pan. Bake at 400 degrees for about 25 minutes, basting frequently with pickle juice.

Mrs. Elaine Wilkinson, Fort Smith, Arkansas

BAKED TURKEY

1 12-lb. frozen turkey	2 stalks celery
Salt to taste	1 med. onion
1/2 lb. butter	

Thaw the turkey. Cut off tips of wings and season inside and out with salt. Place the butter, celery and onion in cavity of the turkey and place turkey in a roasting pan, breast side down. Cover with foil. Roast in 325-degree oven for about 4 hours or until tender. Remove foil and turn turkey. Roast until brown.

Mrs. Fletcher B. White, Erwin, Tennessee

SOUTHERN ROAST TURKEY AND DRESSING

1/2 c. butter	7 c. corn bread crumbs
1/2 c. chopped onion	3 c. cubed bread
1/2 c. diced celery with	2 tbsp. chopped parsley
leaves	4 eggs, beaten
1 1/2 tsp. salt	1 12-lb. turkey
1/2 tsp. poultry seasoning	

Melt the butter in a saucepan. Add the onion, celery, salt and poultry seasoning and cook until onion is tender. Add corn bread crumbs, bread cubes, parsley, eggs and enough water to moisten and mix well. Place in cavity of turkey. Place the turkey in a roasting pan and cover. Bake at 325 degrees for 5 hours or until turkey is tender.

Mrs. Leavy Owens, Tioga, Louisiana

TURKEY AND VEGETABLE PIE

1 pkg. frozen peas	3/4 c. turkey broth
1 pkg. frozen mixed vegetables	3/4 c. milk
2 tbsp. shortening	Salt and pepper to taste
1 onion, diced	2 c. cooked cubed turkey
1 1/2 tbsp. flour	1 recipe unbaked biscuits

Cook the peas and mixed vegetables according to package directions and drain. Melt the shortening in a saucepan. Add the onion and cook until tender. Add flour and stir well. Add the broth and milk and cook until thickened, stirring constantly. Add the salt, pepper, turkey, peas and mixed vegetables and pour into greased baking dish. Cover with biscuits. Bake at 425 degrees for 30 minutes. 6 servings.

Lucy Speck, West Helena, Arkansas

Turkey Pilau (below)

TURKEY PILAU

6 slices bacon	4 1/2 c. turkey broth
1 lge. green pepper, chopped	2 1/3 c. rice
1 med. onion, chopped	3/4 tsp. hot sauce
1 10-oz. package frozen	1 1-lb. 3-oz. can whole
cut okra, thawed	tomatoes
3 tsp. salt	3 c. cooked turkey pieces

Saute the bacon in a skillet until golden. Remove from skillet and break into pieces. Drain off all except 2 tablespoons bacon drippings from the skillet. Add the green pepper, onion, okra and 1 teaspoon salt and saute for about 5 minutes. Bring the turkey broth to a boil in a large saucepan. Add the rice, remaining salt and hot sauce and top with onion mixture. Add the bacon and tomatoes and cover. Simmer for about 25 minutes or until liquid is absorbed. Toss with turkey. Fluff the rice with a fork just before serving. 6 servings.

TURKEY SPOONBREAD

1 c. cornmeal	1/3 c. butter
2 tbsp. tapioca	5 eggs, separated
1 tbsp. salt	4 c. chopped turkey
5 c. turkey broth	

Combine the cornmeal, tapioca, salt and broth in top of a double boiler and cook over boiling water until thick, stirring constantly. Stir in the butter and cool slightly. Beat the egg yolks well and blend in the cornmeal mixture. Add the turkey and mix. Beat egg whites until stiff peaks form and fold into turkey mixture. Place in a greased casserole. Bake at 350 degrees until brown. Serve with giblet gravy, if desired. 12 servings.

Mrs. Frank Slater, Sherman, Texas

ARROZ CON POLLO

1 fryer	1 20-oz. can tomatoes
1 tsp. monosodium glutamate	1 16-oz. can peas
1 1/2 tsp. salt	2 bouillon cubes
1/2 tsp. paprika	1/4 tsp. saffron
1/4 c. olive oil	1 1/2 c. rice
1 med. onion, chopped	

Cut the fryer in serving pieces and sprinkle with monosodium glutamate, 1 teaspoon salt and paprika. Brown in hot oil in a skillet, then place in a baking dish. Add the onion to skillet and cook until tender. Drain the liquid from tomatoes and peas and add enough water to make 3 cups liquid. Stir into skillet, scraping brown particles from bottom of pan. Add the bouillon cubes, saffron and remaining salt and bring to a boil. Pour over the chicken. Sprinkle rice around chicken and stir to moisten rice. Add the tomatoes and cover tightly. Bake in 350-degree oven for 25 minutes. Uncover and fluff the rice. Add the peas and cover. Bake for 10 minutes longer.

Mrs. Martha Livingston, Leesville, Louisiana

BREAST OF CHICKEN PERIGOURDINE

1/2 c. butter or margarine	1/4 tsp. salt
8 boned skinned chicken	1/3 c. flour
breasts	1 1/2 c. chicken broth
8 lge. mushrooms, sliced	1/4 c. light cream

Melt 6 tablespoons butter in a large skillet and add the chicken breasts. Cook over medium heat until browned, then remove from skillet. Place remaining butter in skillet and add mushrooms. Cook over medium heat until golden and remove from skillet with a slotted spoon. Stir salt and flour into drippings in the skillet until blended. Stir in the chicken broth and cream and cook over medium heat, stirring, until thickened and smooth. Place chicken and mushrooms in sauce and cover. Simmer for 20 minutes or until tender.

Susan Hardin, Itasca, Texas

CHICKEN A LA KING

1 can pimento	3 c. milk
1 lge. can mushrooms	1 1/2 tsp. salt
1 green pepper, chopped	1/2 tsp. paprika
6 tbsp. butter	1 cooked chicken, diced
6 tbsp. flour	1 tsp. nutmeg (opt.)

Drain and chop the pimento and mushrooms. Cook the green pepper in the butter in a saucepan until tender. Stir in the flour and mix well. Stir in the milk and cook, stirring constantly, until thickened. Add the pimento, mushrooms and remaining ingredients and heat through. Serve on toast or in timbales. 8 servings.

Antoinette Kelemen, Shelbyville, Kentucky

CHICKEN CREOLE

1 lge. cooked fryer	3 tbsp. flour
1/4 c. margarine	3 tbsp. chili powder
3/4 c. chopped celery	1 tsp. salt
3/4 c. chopped bell pepper	1 can tomatoes, mashed
3/4 c. chopped onion	1 can tomato sauce
3 cloves of garlic, chopped	

Remove bones from fryer and discard skin and bones. Cut the fryer in bite-sized pieces. Heat the margarine in a large saucepan. Add the celery, bell pepper, onion and garlic and cook over medium heat until just tender. Add the flour, chili powder and salt and mix well. Add the tomatoes and tomato sauce and cook until sauce is of medium consistency. Add the chicken and simmer until chicken is heated through. Let stand for several hours to blend flavors, if desired, then reheat. Serve with rice.

Mrs. B. L. Brown, Greenville, Mississippi

CHICKEN CROQUETTES

3 tbsp. butter	1 sm. onion, chopped fine
3 tbsp. flour	Salt and pepper to taste
1 c. milk	Celery salt to taste
1 1/2 c. chopped cooked chicken	1 egg, beaten
	Fine bread crumbs

Melt the butter in top of a double boiler and blend in flour. Add the milk and cook over boiling water until thick and smooth. Add remaining ingredients except egg and crumbs and mix well. Chill. Shape into patties and dip in egg, then in crumbs. Fry in deep, hot fat until brown. 6-8 servings.

Barbara Skinner, Baird, Texas

CHICKEN HASH

2 tbsp. butter or chicken fat	1 c. chicken stock
1 1/2 tbsp. flour	2 c. chopped cooked chicken

Melt the butter in a saucepan and blend in the flour. Add the chicken stock gradually and cook, stirring constantly until mixture comes to a boil. Add the chicken and place in a greased casserole. Bake in a 350-degree oven for 20 minutes. Serve on toast, if desired. 4-6 servings.

Mrs. Beth Moore, Rossville, Georgia

CHICKEN GIBLET JAMBALAYA

6 chicken gizzards	1 c. rice
6 chicken livers	1 tsp. salt (opt.)
1/2 c. chopped onion	1/2 tsp. hot sauce
1/2 c. cooking oil	

Cook the gizzards in boiling, salted water until tender. Drain and reserve 1 1/2 cups broth. Grind the gizzards and livers in a food chopper with coarse blade.

Cook the onion in the oil in a skillet until soft but not brown. Remove from skillet. Add the rice to the skillet and cook, stirring, until light brown. Add the reserved chicken broth and salt and mix well. Add the gizzards, livers, onion and hot sauce and stir. Cover. Cook over low heat for 30 minutes. Remove cover and cook for 10 minutes longer.

Mrs. Helen Wills, New Orleans, Louisiana

CHICKEN AND OLIVES IN CREAM

3 chicken breasts	1 c. heavy cream
1/4 c. butter or margarine	1/3 c. sliced pimento-stuffed
Salt and white pepper	olives
to taste	2 tbsp. chopped parsley
1/4 c. chicken broth	Hot cooked rice or noodles
1/4 c. dry vermouth	

Skin, bone and split the chicken breasts. Heat the butter in a large skillet with a heatproof handle until melted. Turn chicken pieces in butter until coated on all sides. Sprinkle with salt and pepper and cover with a piece of buttered aluminum foil. Bake in 400-degree oven for 30 minutes or until chicken is firm to the touch. Remove chicken and place on a serving platter. Keep warm. Add the broth and vermouth to butter in skillet and cook until half the liquid is evaporated. Stir in the cream and olives and simmer until thickened. Season with salt and pepper and pour over chicken. Sprinkle with parsley and garnish with additional sliced olives, if desired. Serve with rice. Wrap handle in several layers of aluminum foil if skillet does not have heatproof handle. 6 servings.

Chicken and Olives in Cream (above)

CHICKEN LOAF

4 c. cooked diced chicken	1 1/2 tsp. salt
2 c. bread crumbs	3 c. milk or chicken broth
1 c. cooked rice	4 eggs, well beaten

Mix all ingredients and place in a 13 x 9-inch baking pan. Bake at 325 degrees for 1 hour. Serve with mushroom sauce, if desired.

Mrs. A. R. Caldwell, Pocahontas, Arkansas

CHICKEN NEW ORLEANS

6 chicken breast halves	6 lge. mushrooms
1/4 c. cooking oil	1/2 tsp. paprika
1 lge. green pepper, thinly sliced	1/2 c. toasted slivered almonds

Brown the chicken in oil in a skillet over medium heat. Add the green pepper slices and cover. Cook over low heat for 10 minutes. Add the mushrooms and cook for 8 to 10 minutes. Sprinkle with paprika and almonds.

Betty Neff Dickens, Ft. Lauderdale, Florida

CHICKEN-SPANISH OLIVE CASSEROLE

1 tsp. coriander seed	6 whole peppercorns
1/4 tsp. cumin seed	1 tsp. oregano leaves
1 6-lb. chicken, disjointed	3 c. water
2 med. onions, chopped	2 slices bread, cubed
1/2 c. chopped green pepper	1 6-oz. can tomato paste
1/4 c. chopped stuffed olives	1/2 c. golden seedless raisins
2 tsp. salt	1/4 c. sliced stuffed olives
1 stick cinnamon	

Tie the coriander and cumin seed in a cheesecloth bag. Place the chicken, onions, green pepper, chopped olives, salt, cinnamon, peppercorns, oregano and herb bag in a large kettle. Add the water and cover. Simmer for about 50 minutes or until chicken is tender. Remove the chicken from the kettle and cool. Remove chicken from bones and cut in large pieces. Remove the cinnamon, peppercorns and oregano from the kettle and discard. Pour the mixture in the kettle through a coarse sieve and mash the onion mixture through the sieve. Add the bread, tomato paste, raisins, sliced olives and chicken and place in a casserole. Bake at 400 degrees until brown.

Mrs. George E. Jackson, Savannah, Tennessee

FRIED CHICKEN

2 fryers	1/2 c. shortening
Seasoned flour	

Cut the fryers in serving pieces and place in a bag with seasoned flour. Shake bag until fryer pieces are coated, then remove chicken from bag. Melt the shortening in a heavy skillet. Add the chicken and cook until brown on all sides. Reduce heat and cover. Cook for 45 minutes longer or until chicken is tender. Drain on paper towels.

Mrs. Ann Dickinson, Birmingham, Alabama

JUNIPER-SEASONED BROILER

4 tbsp. butter	1 2 1/2-lb. broiler
10 to 12 dried juniper	3/4 c. light cream
berries, crushed	1 1/2 tbsp. flour
1/2 bay leaf, crumbled	1 c. chicken stock
Salt and pepper	2 tbsp. grated cheese

Mix 2 tablespoons butter with juniper berries, bay leaf, 1 teaspoon salt and 1/4 teaspoon pepper and spread on inside of the broiler. Truss the broiler. Brown remaining butter in a Dutch oven. Add the broiler and brown on all sides. Cover. Bake at 350 degrees for about 50 minutes. Remove chicken and keep warm. Add the cream to Dutch oven, small amount at a time. Mix the flour with small amount of water and stir into the cream. Add the chicken stock and cook over low heat for several minutes. Stir in the cheese and salt and pepper to taste. Serve with the chicken.

Juniper-Seasoned Broiler (above)

COQ AU VIN

1 fryer, disjointed	**1 slice ham, diced**
Flour	**1 clove of garlic, minced**
1 stick butter	**Pinch of thyme**
8 to 10 scallions, chopped	**Salt and pepper to taste**
8 to 10 mushrooms	**1 c. red Burgundy**

Dredge the chicken with flour and brown in butter in a skillet. Add the scallions, mushrooms, ham, garlic, thyme, salt, pepper and Burgundy and pour into casserole. Cover. Bake at 350 degrees for 1 hour. Cool and refrigerate for 24 hours. Bake at 300 degrees for 1 hour. 4-6 servings.

Mrs. Leonard McCall, Panama City, Florida

PETIT POIS-CHICKEN PIE

1/2 c. butter	**1/2 can peas, drained**
1/2 c. flour	**2 pimentos, chopped**
2 c. milk	**3 hard-boiled eggs, chopped**
2 c. chicken broth	**1 recipe pastry for 2-crust pie**
2 c. diced cooked chicken	

Melt the butter in a saucepan and stir in the flour. Add the milk and broth and cook, stirring, until thickened. Add the chicken, peas, pimentos and eggs and mix well. Line a shallow baking dish with pastry and pour in chicken mixture. Cover with pastry. Bake at 375 degrees for 30 minutes.

Katherine Kelley, Martinsville, Virginia

ROAST CAPON DELUXE

1 4 to 5-lb. capon or hen	**1 orange, peeled**
2 tbsp. brandy	**1 med. onion, peeled**
Salt	**7 whole cloves**
1 lemon, peeled	**2 tbsp. butter**

Rub cavity of the capon with brandy, then season with salt. Place the lemon and orange in the cavity. Stud the onion with cloves and place in cavity. Truss with skewers. Rub outside of capon with butter and wrap in foil. Place in a baking pan. Roast at 350 degrees for 1 hour and 45 minutes to 2 hours. Fold foil back and roast until brown.

Mrs. Harold Fancher, Montgomery, Alabama

STEWED CHICKEN AND DUMPLINGS

1 4 to 5-lb. chicken, disjointed	**3 tsp. baking powder**
2 1/2 tsp. salt	**3/4 c. milk**
1 1/2 c. all-purpose flour	**1 tsp. minced parsley**

Place the chicken in a kettle and add 2 teaspoons salt. Cover with water and heat to boiling point. Reduce heat and cover. Simmer for 2 hours and 30 minutes to 3 hours or until tender. Remove cover. Sift the flour with baking powder and remaining salt. Add the milk and stir until dry ingredients are moistened. Add parsley and stir until mixed. Add several spoons chicken broth and mix. Drop from a spoon into chicken broth and simmer for 12 minutes. Remove dumplings to a platter and place chicken around dumplings. Pour liquid into a gravy boat and serve with chicken mixture. 6 servings.

Mrs. Virgie Jones, Alpha, Kentucky

PEPPERED CHICKEN WITH CHANTERELLES

2 chickens	**1 lge. onion, finely chopped**
1/4 c. margarine	**1 sm. red bell pepper, chopped**
Salt and pepper to taste	**1 tbsp. flour**
2 c. chanterelles or sliced	**1 c. chicken stock**
mushrooms	**2 tsp. soy sauce**

Cut the chickens in serving pieces and brown in margarine in a skillet over low heat. Remove from skillet and season with salt and pepper. Saute the chanterelles, onion and red pepper in margarine remaining in the skillet until tender. Sprinkle with the flour and add the chicken pieces. Stir in the stock and the soy sauce and bring to a boil. Reduce heat and simmer for 5 minutes. Season with salt and pepper and cover. Let stand for 10 minutes to blend flavors.

Peppered Chicken with Chanterelles (above)

83

Seafood in Croustille (page 94)

creole seafood

Seafood is central to Creole cookery. Some of the earliest Creole recipes used the natural bounty of lakes, marshes, streams, and the Gulf. These fish and shellfish were transformed into dishes that became internationally famed for their savory goodness and tantalizing flavors. People who visited New Orleans frequently made it a point to seek out restaurants featuring these specialties.

Now recipes for some of the most popular Creole seafood dishes are yours in the pages that follow. Discover for yourself the jambalayas, those particularly Creole dishes that combine bits of seafood, meat, vegetables, and rice with hot and zesty seasonings. Crab Jambalaya, Shrimp Jambalaya, and others await you in these pages. Here, too, are recipes for Oysters Rockefeller and Shrimp Arnaud, more famed seafood dishes Creole in origin.

Fish have been incorporated into great dishes, too, as evidenced by the recipe for Pompano Papillotte. In this dish, fish is poached, topped with a complementary sauce, and baked in its own envelope. Baked Creole Red Snapper is a mouth-watering way to prepare a popular Gulf sport fish.

These are just some of the unusual dishes you'll discover as you browse through this treasury of the great Creole fish and shellfish dishes. Make some of them your specialty — and bring yourself a well-deserved reputation as a great cook of seafood!

BAKED CLAMS

1/2 sm. onion, sliced thin	Salt and pepper to taste
1 doz. medium clams on half shell	4 tsp. vinegar

Place an onion slice on each clam and sprinkle each with salt and pepper. Pour 1/3 teaspoon vinegar over each clam and place clams on a baking sheet. Bake at 350 degrees until heated through.

Mrs. O'Rilla Phelps, Supply, North Carolina

FRIED RAZOR CLAMS

6 lge. razor clams	1/4 c. milk
1/2 c. flour	1/2 tsp. salt
2 eggs, lightly beaten	3/4 c. cooking oil

Place the clams and flour in a paper bag and shake to coat clams. Remove clams from bag, shaking off excess flour. Combine the eggs, milk and salt in a bowl and dip the clams in egg mixture. Fry in hot oil in a skillet for about 2 minutes on each side or until lightly browned. Drain on absorbent paper.

Mrs. Irving Thatcher, Shreveport, Louisiana

LOBSTER A LA NEWBURG

2 lb. cooked lobster	Salt and cayenne pepper to taste
1/4 c. melted butter	
1/3 c. sherry	Dash of nutmeg
1 c. cream	2 egg yolks, well beaten

Cut the lobster into large pieces and cook in butter in a saucepan over very low heat for 3 minutes. Add the sherry and cook for 1 minute. Stir in the cream, salt, cayenne pepper and nutmeg. Stir small amount into the egg yolks, then stir back into the lobster mixture. Cook, stirring, until thickened. Serve on toast. 4 servings.

Mrs. M. B. Harper, St. Joseph, Louisiana

LOBSTER THERMIDOR

4 6 to 8-oz. frozen lobster-tails	1 tsp. grated onion
Vinegar	1 tsp. salt
4 tbsp. butter	1/2 tsp. celery salt
4 tbsp. flour	Dash of cayenne pepper
1/2 tsp. prepared mustard	2 egg yolks, slightly beaten
1 1/2 c. milk	2 tsp. lemon juice
1 c. heavy cream	1/4 to 1/3 c. sherry
	Buttered crumbs

Drop the lobster-tails into boiling water, adding 1 tablespoon vinegar for each quart of water, and boil for 9 to 11 minutes. Drain and plunge into cold water.

Remove lobster from shells and cut into small pieces. Reserve shells. Melt the butter in a saucepan over low heat and blend in the flour. Add the mustard and remove from heat. Add the milk gradually, then cook, stirring constantly, until thickened. Add the cream, onion, salt, celery salt and cayenne pepper. Stir small amount into egg yolks, then stir back into remaining sauce. Cook until thick, stirring constantly. Stir in the lemon juice, sherry and lobster. Fill reserved shells with lobster mixture and cover with buttered crumbs. Broil until light brown. 4 servings.

Celia Stansbury, Asheville, North Carolina

ROCK LOBSTER JELLIED IN SHELL

3 9-oz. packages frozen
   South African rock
   lobster-tails
4 env. unflavored gelatin
1/2 c. cold water
3 c. tomato juice

2 3-oz. packages cream
   cheese, softened
1 c. mayonnaise
1/4 c. lemon juice
2 c. chicken broth
Pimento strips

Drop the lobster-tails into boiling, salted water and bring to a boil. Cook for 2 to 3 minutes, then drain immediately. Drench with cold water and cut away under-side membrane. Pull out lobster and dice. Reserve the shells. Soak the gelatin in cold water in a saucepan for 5 minutes. Place over low heat and stir until dissolved. Beat the tomato juice into the cream cheese in a bowl gradually. Beat in the mayonnaise and lemon juice, then beat in the chicken broth gradually. Stir in the gelatin and lobster and chill until slightly thickened. Stir until blended and spoon into reserved lobster shells. Chill until firm. Place on a platter and garnish with pimento strips. Any remaining gelatin mixture may be placed in a small, decorative mold, chilled until firm and used to decorate the platter. 12 servings.

Rock Lobster Jellied in Shell (above)

87

CRAB IMPERIAL

4 tbsp. butter	2 2/3 c. cooked flaked crab
4 tbsp. flour	meat
Juice of 1/2 lemon	2 hard-boiled eggs, minced
1 tsp. prepared mustard	1 tbsp. minced green pepper
1 tsp. horseradish	1 tbsp. Worcestershire sauce
1 tsp. salt	1 c. soft bread crumbs
1 c. milk	Buttered crumbs

Melt the butter in a saucepan and blend in the flour. Add the lemon juice, mustard, horseradish, salt and milk and cook over low heat, stirring constantly, until thickened. Fold in the crab meat, eggs, green pepper and Worcestershire sauce and mix well. Stir in the soft bread crumbs. Place in a baking dish and cover with buttered crumbs. Bake at 400 degrees for 10 minutes or until brown.

Mrs. Andrew Sienkiewicz, Fayetteville, North Carolina

CRAB JAMBALAYA

1/2 c. chopped bacon	1/4 c. rice
1/2 c. chopped onion	1 tbsp. Worcestershire sauce
1/2 c. chopped celery	1/2 tsp. salt
1/2 c. chopped green pepper	Dash of pepper
1 1-lb. 13-oz. can tomatoes	1 lb. cooked crab meat

Fry the bacon in a large saucepan until light brown. Add the onion, celery and green pepper and cook until tender. Add the tomatoes, rice, Worcestershire sauce and seasonings and cover. Simmer for 20 to 25 minutes or until rice is tender, stirring occasionally. Add the crab meat and heat through. 6 servings.

Mrs. Margaret Hodgins, Mobile, Alabama

DEVILED CRAB

2 tbsp. chopped onion	1/2 tsp. sage
4 tbsp. melted butter	1 tbsp. lemon juice
2 tbsp. flour	1 egg, beaten
3/4 c. milk	1 tbsp. chopped parsley
1/2 tsp. salt	1 lb. flaked crab meat
Pepper to taste	1/4 c. bread crumbs
1 tsp. Worcestershire sauce	

Cook the onion in 3 tablespoons butter in a saucepan until tender and blend in the flour. Add the milk gradually and cook until thick, stirring constantly. Add seasonings and lemon juice and mix. Stir small amount of the hot sauce into the egg, then stir back into the sauce. Add the parsley and crab meat and mix. Place in 6 well-greased baking shells. Combine the bread crumbs and remaining butter and sprinkle over top. Place on a baking sheet. Bake at 350 degrees for 15 to 20 minutes or until brown. 5-6 servings.

Mrs. M. H. Long, Cary, North Carolina

SHELLFISH TRIO

1 stalk celery, cut in pieces	2 tbsp. Worcestershire sauce
1/3 c. chopped onion	Hot sauce to taste
6 to 8 peppercorns	Pepper to taste
1 bay leaf	2 tbsp. grated onion
Salt	2 tbsp. horseradish
2 lb. jumbo shrimp	3 doz. clams in shells
3 lemon slices	1 c. cornmeal
1 c. catsup	3 doz. large oysters on half shell
1/2 c. chili sauce	French bread
1/4 c. lemon juice	

Place 2 quarts water, celery, chopped onion, peppercorns, bay leaf and 1 table-spoon salt in a large saucepan and bring to a boil. Add the shrimp and lemon slices and bring to a boil. Reduce heat and simmer for 10 minutes. Cool. Drain the shrimp and remove shells, leaving tails intact. Chill the shrimp. Mix the catsup, chili sauce, lemon juice, Worcestershire sauce, hot sauce, 1/2 teaspoon salt, pepper, grated onion and horseradish in a bowl. Cover and chill. Place the clams in a large container of water and sprinkle with cornmeal. Let stand for at least 4 hours. Clams will absorb cornmeal and work out any sand. Wash and scrub the clams and cover with ice until ready to cook. Place the clams on a grill over hot coals. Cook for about 12 minutes or until shells open. Place the oysters, clams and shrimp on a bed of ice in a serving dish and serve with the cocktail sauce and French bread. May be served with additional lemon juice and horseradish, if desired.

Shellfish Trio (above)

FRIED SOFT-SHELLED CRAB

Soft-shelled crabs	Milk
Salt and pepper to taste	Flour
Lemon juice to taste	Tartar sauce

Drop the crabs into boiling, salted water to cover and cook for about 2 minutes or until crabs are pink. Drain and wash under running water until sand is removed. Place on a board, shell side down, and slice each crab crosswise just back of the eyes. Lift the apron at opposite end and scrape off spongy portion. Cut off the apron. Remove the sand bag. Lift each point at the sides and remove the gills. Wash and dry. Sprinkle with salt, pepper and lemon juice. Dip in milk, then in flour. Fry in deep fat at 370 degrees until brown. Serve with tartar sauce.

Mrs. Sandra Pirtling, Columbus, Mississippi

CREOLE OYSTERS

1 qt. oysters	1/2 tsp. marjoram
2 carrots, chopped	1 bay leaf
2 med. onions, chopped	1 tsp. salt
3 stalks celery, chopped	1 c. light cream
1/2 c. butter	2 tbsp. tomato paste
2 tbsp. parsley	2 tbsp. flour
1 tsp. paprika	2 tbsp. cognac (opt.)
1/2 tsp. thyme	

Drain the oysters and reserve liquid. Saute the carrots, onions and celery in butter in a large saucepan until limp. Add the reserved oyster liquid and cook until most of the liquid evaporates. Add the parsley, paprika, thyme, marjoram, bay leaf and salt and simmer until vegetables are tender, adding water, if needed. Add the oysters and simmer until edges of oysters curl. Add the cream and tomato paste. Mix the flour with 2 tablespoons water, then stir into the oyster mixture. Cook and stir until thickened. Add the cognac and serve. 8 servings.

Mrs. William D. Skinner, Zephyrhills, Florida

OYSTERS IMPROMPTU

1 bunch green onions, chopped	2 pt. oysters, partially drained
1/2 bunch parsley, chopped	1/2 tsp. hot sauce
1/2 c. melted butter	1 1/2 c. bread crumbs

Saute the onions and parsley in butter in a saucepan until limp. Add the oysters and cook until edges of oysters curl. Add the hot sauce and bread crumbs and place in a chafing dish. Keep hot.

Mrs. T. Warren Ogden, Baton Rouge, Louisiana

OYSTERS ROCKEFELLER

Coarse salt	4 slices cooked bacon,
24 oysters on half shell	crumbled

1 c. finely chopped cooked
    spinach
4 tsp. finely chopped parsley
3 celery hearts, finely
    chopped
Top of 1 green onion, finely
    chopped

1/2 tsp. salt
1/8 tsp. cayenne
1/8 tsp. paprika
4 tbsp. melted butter
3 tbsp. lemon juice
2 tbsp. cracker crumbs

Place 1 inch of coarse salt in shallow baking pans and heat. Arrange the oysters over salt. Broil until edges of oysters curl. Combine remaining ingredients in a saucepan and bring to a boil. Spoon over each oyster. Broil until lightly browned.

Shirley Colvin, Alexandria, Louisiana

ROE CASSEROLE WITH A CRAWFISH FLAVOR

1 can cod roe
3 anchovy fillets
3 eggs, well beaten
1 1/4 c. milk

Salt and pepper to taste
Chopped dill
Sliced tomatoes

Mix the roe and the anchovy fillets in a bowl. Mix the eggs and milk and season with salt and pepper. Add 3 tablespoons dill and stir into the roe mixture. Pour into a greased casserole. Bake at 400 degrees for about 35 minutes or until firm. Garnish with sliced tomatoes and chopped dill. 4 servings.

Roe Casserole with a Crawfish Flavor (above)

CRAWFISH PIE

1/4 c. minced celery	1 1/4 c. water
1 bunch shallots, chopped fine	1 can cream of mushroom soup
1/2 sm. green pepper, minced	1 bay leaf
1/4 c. olive oil	Worcestershire sauce to taste
3 c. cooked crawfish tails and fat	4 hard-boiled egg yolks, grated
Salt and pepper to taste	3 slices well-buttered bread
3 drops of hot sauce	Paprika
3 c. cooked rice	

Saute the celery, shallots and green pepper in olive oil in a saucepan for about 5 minutes. Add the crawfish tails and fat and saute for 5 minutes longer. Add the salt, pepper, hot sauce, rice, water, mushroom soup, bay leaf and Worcestershire sauce and mix well. Pour into a greased baking dish and sprinkle egg yolks over the top. Remove the crust from bread and cut each slice into 4 triangles. Arrange the triangles in a circle on top of baking dish and sprinkle with paprika. Bake in a 350-degree oven for about 30 minutes or until heated through and bread is toasted. Garnish with pimento strips. 8 servings.

Mrs. Thad Logan, Gadsden, Alabama

CRAWFISH BISQUE

4 doz. crawfish	1 egg, well beaten
3 slices bread, crumbled	Flour
Milk	1/4 c. olive or salad oil
3 lge. onions, finely chopped	1 can tomato paste
1/4 c. bacon drippings	8 c. hot water
1/4 c. green onion tops	2 bay leaves
5/8 c. chopped parsley	1 tsp. thyme
Salt and pepper to taste	Cayenne pepper to taste
1 tsp. cinnamon	1 lemon, thinly sliced
1/2 tsp. allspice	2 hard-boiled eggs, minced
4 cloves of garlic, minced	2 tbsp. sherry (opt.)

Wash the crawfish thoroughly and place in enough boiling water to cover for 10 minutes. Drain and cool. Separate the heads from the tails and clean the heads, reserving fat. Remove shells from the tails. Place the bread in a small bowl and cover with milk. Let soak. Brown 2 onions in bacon drippings in a large saucepan until tender, then add the crawfish tails. Squeeze the bread dry and add to onion mixture. Add the onion tops, 2 tablespoons parsley, salt, pepper, cinnamon, allspice and 2 cloves of garlic and cook over low heat for several minutes, stirring frequently. Remove from heat and cool slightly. Stir in the beaten egg. Stuff the crawfish heads with the onion mixture, then roll in flour. Fry in the oil in a kettle for about 5 minutes, then remove from kettle. Add 1/2 cup flour to the oil and cook, stirring, until dark brown. Add remaining onions and cook over low heat until translucent. Add any remaining crawfish dressing and tomato paste and mix well. Add the water, salt, pepper, remaining parsley, bay leaves, remaining garlic, thyme and cayenne pepper and bring to a boil. Reduce heat and add the stuffed crawfish heads. Simmer for about 1 hour or until thick, adding water, if needed. Add the lemon and boiled eggs and simmer for 5 minutes. Remove from heat and stir in the sherry. Let stand for 10 minutes.

Mrs. Glenn Whitehead, Columbus, Georgia

BOILED SHRIMP

1 box shrimp and crab boil	Juice of 2 lemons
1 tbsp. salt	2 qt. boiling water
1 lge. onion, chopped	5 lb. shrimp

Place all ingredients in a kettle except shrimp and bring to a boil. Add the shrimp and bring to a boil. Cook for about 6 minutes. Drain the shrimp and cool. Peel and devein the shrimp and place in a bowl. Cover and chill.

Mary Alice O'Brien, Russellville, Arkansas

SHRIMP KABOBS

3 lb. cooked fresh or frozen shrimp	2 tbsp. vinegar
	1 tsp. dry mustard
3 med. green peppers	1/2 tsp. salt
4 med. tomatoes, quartered	1/2 tsp. pepper
1 1/2 c. catsup	1/2 c. chopped onion
1 c. honey	1 clove of garlic, minced
1/4 c. butter or margarine	

Thaw frozen shrimp. Peel and devein the shrimp. Rinse and drain on paper towels. Cut the green peppers into squares. Thread the shrimp alternately with tomato wedges and green pepper squares on 6 long skewers. Combine remaining ingredients in a saucepan and simmer for 10 minutes. Brush kabobs with sauce. Broil about 4 inches from heat for 5 minutes. Baste with sauce. Turn and broil for 5 to 7 minutes longer or until browned, brushing with sauce occasionally.

Shrimp Kabobs (above)

FRENCH-FRIED SHRIMP

1 c. flour	1 c. ice water
1/2 tsp. sugar	2 tbsp. melted shortening or
1 tsp. salt	oil
1 egg	2 lb. shrimp

Combine all ingredients except shrimp in a bowl and beat well. Remove shell from the shrimp, leaving last section and tail intact. Cut slit through center back and remove black line. Dry the shrimp. Dip into batter and fry in deep, hot fat until golden brown. Drain on absorbent paper. Serve hot with tartar sauce. 4-6 servings.

Mabel D. Hickman, Port Isabel, Texas

SEAFOOD IN CROUSTILLE

1/4 c. chopped onion	1 tbsp. Worcestershire sauce
1 c. sliced mushrooms	2 egg yolks, beaten
4 tbsp. butter	2 tsp. sherry
4 tbsp. flour	2 c. cooked lobster, cut in
1/2 tsp. salt	lge. pieces
1/8 tsp. pepper	2 c. cooked cleaned shrimp,
1/8 tsp. paprika	cut in lge. pieces
1 c. cream	12 patty shells
1 c. chicken broth	

Saute the onion and mushrooms in butter in a blazer pan over low heat until onion is tender. Blend in the flour and seasonings and cook until bubbly. Remove from heat. Stir in the cream, broth and Worcestershire sauce and bring to a boil, stirring constantly. Reduce heat and cook for 1 minute. Stir small amount into the egg yolks, then stir back into the blazer pan. Add the sherry, lobster and shrimp and cook for 5 minutes longer, stirring frequently. Place over water pan and keep hot. Serve in patty shells.

Photograph for this recipe on page 84.

ZIPPY SHRIMP AND SPAGHETTI

2 cloves of garlic, minced	1 tsp. dried oregano
1/4 c. cooking oil	1/2 lb. cooked cleaned shrimp
1 16-oz. can tomatoes	1/2 tsp. garlic salt
2 1/2 tsp. salt	1 tsp. prepared horseradish
1/2 tsp. dried basil	1 8-oz. package spaghetti
1 6-oz. can tomato paste	Grated Parmesan cheese

Brown the garlic in oil in a saucepan. Add the tomatoes, salt and basil and simmer for 30 minutes. Stir in the tomato paste and oregano and simmer for 15 minutes. Stir in the shrimp, garlic salt and horseradish and heat through. Cook the spaghetti according to package directions, then drain. Serve the shrimp mixture over spaghetti and sprinkle with cheese. 4 servings.

Elizabeth Miller, Fulton, Mississippi

SHRIMP ORLEANS

1 tbsp. butter or margarine	1 c. sour cream
1 med. onion, sliced	1/4 c. catsup
1 clove of garlic, crushed	1 3-oz. can sliced mushrooms
1 can mushroom soup	2 c. cleaned cooked shrimp

Melt the butter in a saucepan. Add the onion and garlic and cook until onion is tender. Add the soup, sour cream and catsup and mix well. Drain the mushrooms and stir into the soup mixture. Add the shrimp and heat through. Serve over rice.

Mrs. C. W. Cavagnaw, Memphis, Tennessee

PICKLED EEL WITH A TASTE OF CRAWFISH

1 1 1/2-lb. eel, skinned and cleaned	4 tsp. dillseed
4 tomatoes, chopped	1 1/2 tsp. salt
4 tbsp. tomato paste	1 1/4 c. water

Rinse the eel and cut in thin slices. Place in a saucepan. Mix the tomatoes, tomato paste, dillseed, salt and water and pour over the eel. Cover and simmer for about 10 minutes. Add more salt, if needed. Garnish with parsley.

Pickled Eel with a Taste of Crawfish (above)

SHRIMP ARNAUD

1 c. olive oil	1/2 c. Dijon mustard
1/4 c. vinegar	1 tsp. paprika
1/2 c. diced celery	2 lb. cooked cleaned shrimp
1/2 c. diced onion	

Mix all ingredients in a bowl and chill for several hours. Serve on shredded lettuce. 6 servings.

Mrs. R. L. McLendon, Marianna, Florida

SHRIMP AMANDINE

2 lb. cleaned shrimp	1/8 tsp. mace
3/4 c. rice	1 can tomato soup
1/4 c. chopped onions	1 c. light cream
1/4 c. chopped green pepper	1/2 c. sherry
2 tbsp. butter or margarine	1/2 c. blanched slivered
1 tsp. salt	almonds
1/8 tsp. pepper	Paprika

Cook the shrimp in boiling, salted water, covered, for 5 minutes, then drain. Cook the rice according to package directions and cool. Saute the onions and green pepper in butter in a saucepan for 5 minutes. Add the salt, pepper, mace, soup, cream, sherry and 1/4 cup almonds and turn into a 1 1/2-quart casserole. Reserve several shrimp for garnish. Place the rice and remaining shrimp in the casserole and mix. Top with remaining almonds and sprinkle with paprika. Bake at 350 degrees for 30 minutes. Top with reserved shrimp and bake for 10 minutes longer. Garnish with watercress, if desired. 6-8 servings.

Mrs. Mildred F. Publicover, Rockledge, Florida

SHRIMP JAMBALAYA

3 lb. fresh shrimp	1 can tomatoes
Salt and pepper to taste	1 can tomato paste
Red pepper to taste	1 can tomato sauce
1/2 c. cooking oil	1/2 tsp. sugar
1 c. chopped onions	3 c. cooked rice
1 c. chopped celery	Chopped parsley to taste
2 cloves of garlic, minced	Chopped green onions to taste
1/2 c. green pepper, chopped	1 pimento, diced

Cook the shrimp in boiling water with salt, pepper and red pepper for 5 minutes. Let stand for 5 minutes, then drain. Peel and devein the shrimp. Heat the oil in a kettle. Add the onions, celery, garlic and green pepper and cook over medium heat for 15 minutes. Add the tomatoes, tomato paste, tomato sauce and sugar and cook for about 40 minutes. Add the shrimp and cook for 30 minutes. Stir in remaining ingredients and salt and pepper and heat through. 12 servings.

Louise H. Brown, Eau Gallie, Florida

Baked Stuffed Bass (below)

BAKED STUFFED BASS

1/3 c. chopped onion	1 3/4 tsp. salt
1/4 c. chopped parsley	1/8 tsp. pepper
1/2 c. finely chopped celery	1 3 to 4-lb. bass, dressed
1/2 c. melted butter	for stuffing
6 c. soft 1/4-in. bread cubes	

Saute the onion, parsley and celery in 1/3 cup butter in a saucepan until onion is tender. Add the bread cubes, 1/4 teaspoon salt and pepper and stir to coat bread cubes. Brown bread lightly, stirring constantly. Sprinkle remaining salt over inside and outside of the bass. Stuff the bass loosely with bread mixture. Close and secure with skewers. Place in a greased shallow baking dish and brush with remaining butter. Bake in 350-degree oven for 45 to 60 minutes or until fish flakes easily, basting several times with additional butter or pan drippings.

Caper Sauce

2 tbsp. butter	1 1/2 c. milk
1/4 c. chopped onion	2 tbsp. lemon juice
2 tbsp. flour	2 tbsp. drained capers
1/2 tsp. salt	1 tbsp. chopped parsley

Melt the butter in a saucepan. Add the onion and saute until tender. Blend in the flour and salt. Stir in the milk and cook, stirring constantly, until smooth and thickened. Stir in the lemon juice, capers and parsley. Serve with bass.

97

BAKED BASS

1 5-lb. bass	1 tbsp. Worcestershire sauce
Salt and pepper to taste	1 tbsp. catsup
Flour	1 tsp. chili powder
1/2 c. chopped onion	1/2 lemon, thinly sliced
2 c. chopped celery	2 bay leaves
1/4 c. chopped green pepper	1 clove of garlic, minced
6 tbsp. melted butter	Dash of red pepper
3 c. canned tomatoes	

Sprinkle the bass with salt and pepper and dredge with flour. Place in a baking dish. Cook the onion, celery and green pepper in butter in a saucepan for 15 minutes. Add remaining ingredients and simmer for 15 minutes. Place in blender container and blend until pureed. Pour over the bass. Bake at 350 degrees for 45 minutes, basting frequently. 6 servings.

Mrs. Ray Mouser, Tyler, Texas

BAKED BASS WITH SPANISH SAUCE

1 sm. jar pimento strips	1 8-oz. can tomato sauce
1 green pepper, chopped	1 sm. can tiny green peas
1 onion, chopped	1 8-oz. can mushroom
1 clove of garlic, chopped	stems and pieces
2 tbsp. shortening or oil	Salt and pepper to taste
1 No. 2 can tomatoes	4 sm. bass

Drain the pimento strips. Cook the green pepper, onion and garlic in the shortening in a saucepan over medium heat until onion is tender. Add pimento and remaining ingredients except bass and cook over low heat for about 15 minutes or until liquid has evaporated. Line a baking pan with foil, leaving enough to fold over bass. Sprinkle the bass with salt and pepper and place on the foil. Cover with sauce and fold foil over the bass. Seal edges. Bake in 350-degree oven for 1 hour.

Mrs. W. C. Martin, Ocala, Florida

BAKED COD IN LIME JUICE

2 lb. cod fillets	1 tsp. powdered ginger
1 1/2 tsp. salt	1 tsp. grated lemon rind
1/4 tsp. pepper	1/2 bay leaf, crushed
1/2 c. lime juice	2 tbsp. butter
2 tbsp. minced onion	Lime slices

Place the fillets in a baking dish and sprinkle with 1 teaspoon salt and 1/8 teaspoon pepper. Mix remaining salt and pepper and remaining ingredients except butter and lime slices and pour over the fillets. Let stand at room temperature for 1 hour. Dot with butter and place lime slices on top. Bake at 350 degrees for 20 to 25 minutes. 4 servings.

Yvonne Wisby, Roll, Arizona

FISH CROQUETTES

1 c. flaked cooked fish	1 tsp. Worcestershire sauce
1/3 c. mayonnaise	1 tbsp. finely chopped onion
Pepper to taste	1/2 c. soft bread crumbs
1 tbsp. lemon juice	Toasted bread crumbs

Mix the fish with remaining ingredients except toasted bread crumbs and shape into croquettes. Roll in toasted bread crumbs and place in a foil-covered cookie pan. Bake at 450 degrees for 12 to 15 minutes.

Mrs. Tom Caudle, Ballinger, Texas

BAKED FILLET OF FLOUNDER

1 lb. flounder fillets	1/2 c. grated sharp Cheddar
Salt and pepper to taste	cheese
1 tbsp. butter or margarine	Chopped parsley to
1 tbsp. flour	taste (opt.)
1/3 c. milk or light cream	Paprika to taste (opt.)

Place the fillets in a greased shallow casserole and season with salt and pepper. Bake at 375 degrees for 15 minutes. Melt the butter in a saucepan and stir in the flour. Stir in the milk and cook, stirring constantly, until smooth and thick. Add cheese and stir until melted. Remove from heat. Remove fillets from oven and pour off and discard liquid. Spread cheese sauce over fillets and sprinkle with parsley and paprika. Bake for 10 minutes longer.

Mrs. R. D. Cox, New Orleans, Louisiana

BROILED FLOUNDER FILLETS

1 lb. frozen flounder	2 tbsp. lemon juice
fillets, thawed	3 tbsp. butter
1/2 tsp. salt	

Place the fillets in an aluminum foil-lined baking pan and sprinkle with salt and lemon juice. Dot with butter. Broil for 20 minutes or until brown.

Mrs. Clarinda A. Britt, Pensacola, Florida

FRIED FLOUNDER

1 lb. flounder fillets	Paprika to taste
1/3 c. sour cream	Biscuit mix
4 tsp. lemon juice	Cooking oil

Dry the fillets with paper towels. Mix the sour cream, lemon juice and paprika. Dip the fillets in the sour cream mixture, then in biscuit mix, coating well. Place on a cookie sheet and refrigerate for 1 hour or longer. Fry in 1/2 inch oil in a skillet until brown, turning once. Serve with tartar sauce.

Mrs. Arthur Belcher, Saint Petersburg, Florida

STUFFED FLOUNDER

2 tbsp. flour	Dash of hot sauce
Salt to taste	6 tbsp. melted butter or
1 tbsp. mustard	margarine
1 tsp. Worcestershire sauce	2/3 c. milk
4 tsp. lemon juice	2 c. cooked crab meat
Dash of pepper	8 flounder fillets

Stir the flour, salt, mustard, Worcestershire sauce, 1 teaspoon lemon juice, pepper and hot sauce into 4 tablespoons butter in a saucepan. Add milk gradually and cook over low heat, stirring constantly, until thickened. Add the crab meat and mix. Place 4 fillets in a greased shallow baking pan and spread with crab meat mixture. Top with remaining fillets and brush with remaining butter and lemon juice. Bake at 350 degrees for 25 minutes.

Mrs. E. C. Kirkland, Flagstaff, Arizona

BAKED SPANISH MACKEREL

Salad dressing or mayonnaise	Salt to taste
1 1/2 lb. Spanish mackerel	4 tbsp. melted margarine
fillets	Paprika to taste

Line a shallow pan with foil and coat with salad dressing. Place the fillets on the foil, skin side down, and sprinkle with salt. Spread salad dressing over fillets. Pour the margarine over fillets and sprinkle with paprika. Bake at 425 degrees for 15 to 20 minutes.

Mrs. Sam H. Cobb, Citra, Florida

GLORIFIED KING MACKEREL

1 1-lb. king mackerel	1 tbsp. Worcestershire sauce
fillet	1/2 tsp. salt
1/2 c. cooking sauterne	Flour
1/2 tsp. celery salt	Bacon drippings
1/2 tsp. onion salt	Cooking oil

Cut the fillet into 1-inch squares and place in a shallow pan. Combine the sauterne, celery salt, onion salt, Worcestershire sauce and salt and pour over the mackerel. Marinate for 20 minutes. Drain, then dredge with flour. Place equal amounts of bacon drippings and oil in a deep fryer and heat. Fry the mackerel in the oil mixture until brown. Serve immediately.

Mrs. Nancye A. Laine, Suffolk, Virginia

STUFFED MACKEREL

1 onion, diced	1 tbsp. chopped celery
1 tbsp. diced green pepper	2 tbsp. butter

2 c. bread, cut in 1/2-in. cubes
1/2 tsp. poultry seasoning
1/2 tsp. sage

1 lge. Spanish mackerel
2 bacon slices

Saute the onion, green pepper and celery in butter in a saucepan until onion is tender but not brown. Cool. Add the bread cubes and mix. Add the poultry seasoning and sage and mix thoroughly. Stuff the mackerel with dressing and secure opening. Place in a greased baking pan and place the bacon over top. Bake at 350 degrees for 45 minutes.

Mrs. L. A. Washington, Newark, Arkansas

FROGS' LEGS ELEGANTE

1/2 c. butter
1/4 c. olive oil
Juice of 2 lemons
Pressed garlic to taste
1 c. finely chopped parsley

1/2 c. white Rhine wine
Salt and pepper to taste
2 lb. frogs' legs
Flour

Combine all ingredients except frogs' legs and flour in a skillet and heat. Dredge the frogs' legs with flour. Cook in the butter mixture until brown, turning frequently. Serve at once.

Mrs. C. W. Schooley, III, West Palm Beach, Florida

BAKED MULLET FILLETS

2 lb. mullet fillets
1/2 c. French dressing
1 1/2 c. cheese cracker crumbs

2 tbsp. melted oil
Paprika to taste

Skin the fillets and cut into serving portions. Dip in French dressing and coat with cracker crumbs. Place in a well-greased 15 x 12-inch cookie pan and drizzle with oil. Sprinkle with paprika. Bake at 500 degrees for 10 to 12 minutes or until fish flakes easily when tested with a fork. Sprinkle with salt, if desired.

Mrs. R. L. Berry, Little Rock, Arkansas

PERCH PIQUANT

4 onions, sliced
2 lb. perch fillets
1/2 c. mayonnaise
2 tsp. Worcestershire sauce

2 tbsp. lemon juice
1/4 c. grated Parmesan cheese
2 tbsp. chopped parsley

Place the onions in a saucepan and cover with water. Cook until crisp-tender, then drain. Place in a shallow, well-greased baking dish. Cut the perch into serving pieces and place over onions. Combine remaining ingredients and blend well. Spread over the perch. Bake at 350 degrees for 30 to 40 minutes or until fish flakes easily when tested with a fork. Garnish with lemon slices.

Mrs. Hubert Miers, West Palm Beach, Florida

Lemon-Fried Yellow Perch (below)

LEMON-FRIED YELLOW PERCH

2 lb. fresh or frozen	3 eggs, beaten
yellow perch fillets	1 1/2 tsp. salt
1/4 c. lemon juice	1 c. flour

Thaw frozen fillets. Cut the perch into serving portions and place in a shallow baking dish. Pour lemon juice over perch and let stand for 10 minutes, turning once. Combine the eggs and salt. Roll the perch in flour, then dip in eggs. Fry in hot fat in a skillet over moderate heat for 3 to 4 minutes or until brown. Turn carefully and cook for 3 to 4 minutes longer or until brown.6 servings.

POMPANO PAPILLOTE

1 onion, finely chopped	Dash of hot sauce
1/2 c. melted butter	2 tbsp. sauterne
1/2 c. flour	1/2 lb. cooked cleaned shrimp
2 c. scalded milk	1/2 lb. cooked cleaned
2 eggs	crawfish
Dash of nutmeg	Salt to taste
1 tsp. Worcestershire sauce	6 pompano steaks, skinned

Saute the onion in butter in a saucepan for 5 minutes. Stir in the flour. Add the milk slowly and cook until thick, stirring constantly. Beat the eggs with the nutmeg, Worcestershire sauce, hot sauce and sauterne and stir into the milk mixture. Chop the shrimp and crawfish and stir into the sauce. Stir in the salt. Place alternate layers of sauce and pompano on greased parchment paper. Fold paper to form bag with crimped edges and brush additional melted butter over paper. Place in a baking pan. Bake at 350 degrees for 30 minutes. Thin brown paper bag may be substituted for parchment paper.

Jeanette Meadows, Live Oak, Florida

BAKED CREOLE RED SNAPPER

6 slices bread, crumbled	3 c. chopped celery
3 tsp. salt	1 No. 2 can tomatoes
1 1/2 tsp. pepper	6 c. water
Shortening	1 whole clove
1 6 to 8-lb. red snapper,	3 sprigs of parsley
dressed	1 bay leaf
2 lge. onions, chopped	1 sprig of thyme
1 clove of garlic, chopped	

Place the bread in a bowl and cover with water. Let stand for 5 minutes, then squeeze dry. Combine 1 teaspoon salt, 1/2 teaspoon pepper and 1 1/2 table-spoons shortening and rub on inside and outside of snapper. Fry half the onions, bread, 1 teaspoon salt and 1/2 teaspoon pepper in 1/2 cup shortening in a saucepan for 15 minutes, then cool. Stuff the snapper with bread mixture and secure opening. Place in a shallow baking pan. Bake at 400 degrees for 30 minutes. Fry remaining onions, garlic and celery in 1/2 cup shortening in a saucepan until onions are tender. Add remaining salt and pepper and remaining ingredients and pour over the snapper. Reduce temperature to 350 degrees and bake for 30 minutes longer. 10 servings.

Mrs. Chester W. Peeples, Jr., West Memphis, Arkansas

MARINATED RED SNAPPER

1 3 1/2-lb. red snapper,	Seasoned salt
dressed	Paprika
1/2 c. cooking oil	Juice of 1 lemon
1 sm. onion, grated	

Fillet the red snapper and soak in salted water for 1 hour. Drain. Dip the fillets in oil. Place in a shallow dish and sprinkle with onion. Sprinkle with seasoned salt, paprika and lemon juice and refrigerate for 1 hour. Drain and reserve marinade. Place fillets in a shallow baking pan. Broil for 30 minutes, basting with reserved marinade occasionally. 4 servings.

Mrs. J. B. O'Connor, Chattahoochee, Florida

RED SNAPPER AMANDINE

4 6 to 8-oz. red snapper	1/2 tsp. onion juice
fillets	1/2 c. margarine
Salt to taste	1/4 c. blanched slivered almonds
Flour	1 tbsp. lemon juice

Wash and dry the fillets. Sprinkle with salt and dust with flour. Heat the onion juice and half the margarine in a heavy skillet. Add the fillets and cook until light brown. Place in a hot serving dish. Pour margarine from skillet. Add remaining margarine and almonds and cook over low heat until almonds are brown. Add the lemon juice and pour over the fillets.

Patricia Nelson Moon, Bartlesville, Oklahoma

RED SNAPPER CREOLE

1 clove of garlic, minced	1/2 c. water
1/4 c. olive oil	Dash of Worcestershire sauce
1/4 c. butter	Salt and pepper to taste
1 c. chopped onions	Juice of 1/2 lemon
1 sm. can tomato paste	2 c. chopped tomatoes
1 c. chopped celery	8 broiled red snapper fillets
1 c. chopped green peppers	

Heat the garlic in a frying pan with olive oil and butter. Add the onions and cook until onions are light brown. Add the tomato paste, celery, green peppers, water, Worcestershire sauce, seasonings, lemon juice and tomatoes and bring to a boil. Reduce heat and simmer for 1 hour or until sauce is thickened, stirring occasionally. Serve over red snapper.

Mrs. Davis Grimes, Tulsa, Oklahoma

STUFFED RED SNAPPER

1 3-lb. red snapper, dressed	1 1/4 c. crumbled crackers
1/3 c. butter	3 tbsp. melted butter
1 tbsp. flour	1 egg, beaten
2 tbsp. salt	1/2 c. chopped celery
Dash of pepper	2 tbsp. chopped green pepper
3 tbsp. lemon juice	1/2 c. chopped onion
1/4 c. crumbled corn bread or	1 tbsp. chopped parsley
bread	1 tbsp. chopped pimento

Wash and dry the snapper. Cream the butter in a bowl and stir in the flour, salt and pepper. Stir in 2 tablespoons lemon juice. Rub snapper inside and out with butter mixture. Place in a shallow baking pan and cover. Refrigerate for 30 minutes. Place the corn bread and cracker crumbs in a bowl and pour 2/3 cup water over crumbs. Add the melted butter, remaining lemon juice and remaining ingredients and mix well. Stuff the snapper with the onion mixture and secure the opening. Bake at 350 degrees for 1 hour and 30 minutes, basting with small amount of hot water every 20 minutes.

Mrs. Irma Chandler, Dallas, Texas

BAKED REDFISH WITH CORN BREAD DRESSING

1 c. corn bread mix	2 tsp. salt
1 lge. onion, finely chopped	1 tsp. cayenne pepper
2 tbsp. cooking oil	1 8-oz. can tomato sauce
1 3-lb. redfish, drawn and	1 c. cocktail vegetable juice
scaled	

Prepare and bake the corn bread mix according to package directions for corn bread, then cool. Crumble and place in a bowl. Add 1/3 cup water. Saute 1/2 of the onion in the oil in a saucepan until tender, then stir in corn bread. Cool. Remove eyes of redfish and leave head intact. Mix the salt and pepper and rub on outside and inside cavity of the redfish. Stuff the redfish with corn bread mixture and secure opening. Place on a rack in a baking pan. Mix the tomato sauce, vegetable juice and remaining onion and pour over redfish. Bake in 325-degree oven for 1 hour to 1 hour and 15 minutes. Remove to a large platter and garnish with sliced lemon and parsley, if desired. Pour 1/4 cup water into the baking pan and cook over low heat, stirring, until heated through. Serve with redfish.

Mrs. Mathilde M. Cire, Alexandria, Louisiana

SALMON DIVAN PROVENCALE

1 1-lb. can salmon	1/2 tsp. salt
Milk	1/4 tsp. white pepper
2 10-oz. packages frozen	3/4 c. shredded Cheddar
broccoli spears	cheese
4 tbsp. butter	1 1-lb. can tomatoes
1/4 tsp. minced garlic	2 tbsp. buttered bread
5 tbsp. flour	crumbs

Preheat oven to 400 degrees. Drain the salmon and reserve liquid. Add enough milk to reserved liquid to make 1 1/2 cups liquid. Flake the salmon into large chunks and set aside. Prepare the broccoli according to package directions, cooking half as long, then drain thoroughly. Arrange in a shallow 8-inch baking dish and spread the salmon over broccoli. Melt the butter in a saucepan. Add the garlic and flour and cook, stirring, until bubbly. Add the salt and pepper. Stir in the milk mixture gradually and cook, stirring, until thickened. Add the cheese and cook, stirring, until cheese is melted. Drain the tomatoes and cut into chunks. Add to the sauce and pour over the salmon. Sprinkle with bread crumbs. Bake for 20 to 25 minutes or until crumbs are lightly browned.

Salmon Divan Provencale (above)

FRIED FILLET OF SOLE

1/2 c. vegetable shortening	1 tbsp. milk
1 1/2 lb. sole fillets	1 c. fine bread crumbs
Salt and pepper to taste	Lemon wedges
1 egg	

Heat the shortening in a large skillet. Sprinkle the fillets with salt and pepper. Beat the egg with milk. Dip the fillets into egg mixture, then into crumbs. Fry in shortening over medium heat until golden, turning once. Serve with lemon wedges and garnish with parsley. Serve with tartar sauce, if desired.

Betty Gilmore, Tifton, Georgia

SOLE AU GRATIN

2 sole	1 tbsp. tomato paste
2 tbsp. oil	Salt and pepper to taste
2 carrots, chopped	1 1/2 c. stock
2 onions, chopped	2 tbsp. white wine
2 tbsp. flour	1 tbsp. fine bread crumbs
1 tomato, chopped	1 tbsp. grated cheese
1 can mushroom stems and pieces	1 lemon, sliced

Wash and dry the sole and score well. Place in a shallow baking pan. Heat the oil in a saucepan. Add the carrots and onions and cook over low heat until onions are tender. Add the flour and cook until flour is brown. Add tomato, mushrooms, tomato paste, salt, pepper and stock and bring to a boil. Reduce heat and simmer for 20 minutes. Add the wine and pour over the sole. Sprinkle with bread crumbs and cheese. Bake at 400 degrees for 30 minutes or until fish flakes easily when tested with a fork. Garnish with lemon slices.

Mrs. C. W. Holland, Danville, Virginia

FRIED BROOK TROUT

2 lb. pan-dressed brook trout	1 tbsp. milk or water
1 tsp. salt	1 c. bread or cracker crumbs
1/8 tsp. pepper	Melted fat
1 egg, slightly beaten	

Cut the trout into serving portions and sprinkle with salt and pepper. Mix the egg and milk. Dip trout in egg mixture and roll in crumbs. Place 1/8 inch fat in a heavy frying pan and heat. Place the trout in the fat and cook over moderate heat for about 5 minutes or until brown. Turn carefully and cook for 5 minutes longer or until brown. Drain on absorbent paper. May be served with lemon-butter sauce.

Mrs. Ben Stockton, Silver Spring, Maryland

GRILLED TROUT

6 dressed trout	1 tsp. salt
1/4 c. French dressing	1/4 tsp. pepper
1 tbsp. lemon juice	

Wash and dry the trout. Combine remaining ingredients and brush each trout inside and out with French dressing mixture. Place on a well-greased grill. Cook over moderately hot coals for 15 to 20 minutes. Turn and brush with French dressing mixture. Cook for 15 minutes longer or until fish flakes easily when tested with a fork.

Mrs. Maurice Goolsby, Carthage, Texas

GOURMET BROOK TROUT IN CAPER SAUCE

4 12-oz. brook trout	1 tbsp. butter
1 1/2 tsp. seasoned salt	2 tbsp. flour
1/2 c. dry white wine	1/2 c. milk
10 peppercorns	1 1/2 tbsp. chopped capers
1 tsp. instant chicken bouillon	

Sprinkle inside of trout with salt. Place the trout in a large skillet and add the wine, peppercorns and bouillon. Simmer, covered, for 15 minutes or until fish flakes easily when tested with a fork. Cool for 10 minutes. Fillet the trout and remove skin. Place fillets in a lightly-greased baking dish. Strain the stock. Melt the butter in a saucepan, then blend in flour. Cook for 1 minute, stirring constantly. Add the milk and 1 cup stock gradually and cook over low heat, stirring constantly, until thickened. Add the capers and spoon over trout. Bake in 375-degree oven for 20 to 25 minutes or until sauce is bubbly.

Mrs. Olive W. Esser, Mobile, Alabama

TROUT MARGUERY

3 tbsp. flour	1/4 c. dry white wine
6 tbsp. melted butter	6 lb. trout fillets
1 lb. cleaned cooked shrimp, chopped	Salt and cayenne pepper to taste
4 green onions, chopped	Toast
12 oysters, chopped	Chopped parsley

Blend the flour into the butter in a saucepan, then stir in the shrimp. Add the onions and cook until onions are wilted. Add the oysters and simmer for 5 minutes. Stir in the wine and remove from heat. Sprinkle trout with salt and cayenne pepper. Place in a shallow pan and broil until brown. Arrange trout on toast and cover with sauce. Sprinkle with parsley.

Mrs. Janet S. Chatelain, Bunkie, Louisiana

TROUT AMANDINE

1 1 1/2-lb. speckled trout	Toasted slivered almonds
2 eggs, beaten	1/4 c. melted butter
Salt	1/4 tsp. white pepper
Pepper to taste	1 tsp. chopped parsley
Flour	1/2 clove of garlic, minced
1 c. salad oil	

Fillet the trout and remove skin. Dip fillets in eggs and season with salt to taste and pepper. Dredge with flour. Heat the oil in a skillet. Saute the fillets in the oil until brown, turning once. Place on a warm platter and sprinkle with almonds. Mix the butter, 1/4 teaspoon salt, white pepper, parsley and garlic and pour over fillets.

Mrs. A. Henderson, Jackson, Mississippi

STUFFED TROUT

1/4 c. chopped onion	1/2 tsp. sage
6 tbsp. melted butter	2 1-lb. trout, dressed
1/2 c. cracker crumbs	1/2 c. wine
1/2 c. bread crumbs	1/2 lb. small mushrooms
1/4 tsp. salt	

Saute the onions in 3 tablespoons butter in a saucepan until tender. Add cracker and bread crumbs, salt and sage. Stuff the trout with crumb mixture and secure openings. Place in a greased baking dish and cut shallow slits on top. Bake at 400 degrees for 10 minutes. Baste with 2 tablespoons butter and add the wine. Bake for 10 to 15 minutes longer. Saute the mushrooms in remaining butter. Place the trout on a platter. Add trout drippings to mushrooms and spoon over trout.

Charlotte Redhead, Centreville, Mississippi

TURTLE STEAKS

4 med. turtle steaks	1 egg
1/2 tsp. salt	3 tbsp. milk
1/4 tsp. pepper	1 c. flour
Lemon juice	4 tbsp. cooking oil
3 cloves of garlic, thinly sliced	

Sprinkle the steaks with salt and pepper. Place in a shallow dish and cover with lemon juice. Sprinkle with garlic. Marinate for 4 hours. Beat the egg and milk in a bowl. Dip each steak in egg mixture, then coat with flour. Fry in oil in a skillet until dark brown.

Mrs. A. R. Johnson, St. Petersburg, Florida

BAKED WHITEFISH WITH STUFFING

1 3 to 4-lb. whitefish, dressed	Salt and pepper to taste
	2 c. soft bread crumbs

1 c. celery
2 tbsp. minced onion
1 tbsp. minced parsley
4 tbsp. melted butter

2 tbsp. soft butter
2 tbsp. lemon juice
Paprika

Have butcher remove whitefish bones, leaving one side intact. Sprinkle inside and outside of whitefish with salt and pepper. Mix the crumbs, celery, onion, parsley, melted butter and 1/2 cup hot water and place in cavity of the whitefish. Fasten with skewers or sew opening together. Place in pan lined with foil and add 1 cup water. Rub with soft butter and lemon juice and sprinkle with paprika. Bake at 375 degrees for 1 hour to 1 hour and 20 minutes or until fish flakes easily when tested with a fork.

Mrs. B. S. Brown, Kannapolis, North Carolina

BAKED FISH IN SOUR CREAM

1/2 8-oz. package
   herb-seasoned stuffing mix
1 3 to 4-lb. whitefish with
   head and tail, cleaned
1 c. sour cream

1/4 tsp. salt
1/4 tsp. celery salt
1/4 tsp. dillseed
1 tbsp. flour
2 tbsp. chopped onion

Prepare stuffing mix according to package directions for dry stuffing. Place in cavity of the whitefish and lace or skewer opening. Stand the whitefish on underside in a greased baking dish. Combine remaining ingredients and spread over top of whitefish. Bake in 350-degree oven for about 1 hour or until tender and lightly browned. 4-6 servings.

Baked Fish in Sour Cream (above)

Louisiana Yam-Apricot Pudding (page 124)

creole vegetables

Creole homemakers always seemed to realize how important a role vegetables played. Vegetables not only provided important nutrients everyone in the family needed but they lent variety to every menu. Behind almost every Creole kitchen was the family garden where vegetables were lovingly cultivated.

Recipes for these vegetable dishes were an important part of the Creole cuisine. Many home-tested, family-approved recipes are yours in the pages of this section. Plump and purple eggplant was popular fare in Creole homes, and when you prepare Eggplant Crevette Creole, you'll understand why. The subtle blend of seasonings makes this vegetable dish a real treat! Vegetable Stuffed Green Peppers was another favorite Creole dish — and one that was particularly popular during the meatless Lenten days following Mardi Gras!

Explore these pages of unusual vegetable recipes still further and discover how to prepare Creole Green Beans ... Wilted Leaf Lettuce ... Tomatoes Vinaigrette ... and many other sure-to-be-appreciated vegetable recipes. And if okra and sweet potatoes are popular in your house, feature them Creole-style, in Okra Creole or Candied Sweet Potatoes!

Wake up your family's love for well cooked and properly seasoned vegetables. With these delicious recipes, vegetables will never seem ordinary again!

ORLEANIAN ARTICHOKES

4 artichokes	1/4 tsp. garlic juice
Salt	1 tbsp. vinegar
1 3-oz. package cream cheese	3 tbsp. sherry
1 3-oz. package blue cheese	Dash of hot sauce
1 tsp. lemon juice	

Wash the artichokes. Cut off stems at base and remove small bottom leaves. Trim tips of leaves and cut off about 1 inch from top of artichokes. Stand the artichokes upright in a deep saucepan large enough to hold snugly. Add 1 teaspoon salt and 2 to 3 inches boiling water and cover. Simmer for 35 to 45 minutes or until base may be pierced easily with a fork, adding boiling water, if needed. Turn artichokes upside down to drain and cool. Spread leaves gently and remove choke from center of the artichokes with a metal spoon. Place remaining ingredients and salt to taste in a mixing bowl and beat with mixer at high speed until smooth and creamy. Serve with artichokes.

Mrs. Juluis F. Guenther, New Orleans, Louisiana

ASPARAGUS AU GRATIN

2 tbsp. butter	1/2 c. grated sharp American
2 tbsp. flour	cheese
1/4 tsp. salt	2 c. cooked asparagus
1/8 tsp. pepper	1/2 c. blanched slivered
1/4 tsp. dry mustard	almonds
1 c. milk	

Melt the butter in a saucepan and blend in the flour, salt, pepper and mustard. Stir in the milk and cook until thickened, stirring constantly. Remove from heat. Add the cheese and stir until melted. Place alternate layers of asparagus and cheese sauce in a casserole and cover with the almonds. Bake at 350 degrees for 20 minutes. 4-5 servings.

Mrs. Patsy Lynch, Copperhill, Tennessee

GREEN BEAN CASSEROLE

3 c. young green beans	1/4 c. chopped pimento
3 tbsp. butter or margarine	1 8-oz. can tomato sauce
1 clove of garlic, minced	1 tsp. hot sauce
1 med. onion, minced	1 c. shredded Cheddar cheese
1 sm. green pepper, chopped	

Remove string ends from the beans and slice beans in half, if desired. Cook the beans in a small amount of water until just tender, then drain. Melt the butter in a 1-quart saucepan. Add the garlic, onion, green pepper and pimento and saute for about 5 minutes. Stir in the tomato sauce, hot sauce and beans. Turn into a 1-quart casserole and sprinkle with cheese. Bake in 350-degree oven for about 25 minutes. About 4 servings.

CREOLE GREEN BEANS AND TOMATOES

1 med. onion, chopped	1/4 tsp. salt
3 tbsp. chopped green pepper	1/8 tsp. pepper
2 tbsp. margarine	3 c. cooked green beans
2 1/2 c. tomatoes	2 tbsp. flour
1/4 tsp. thyme	2 tbsp. water
1 tsp. sugar	

Saute the onion and green pepper in the margarine in a saucepan until tender. Add the tomatoes, thyme, sugar, salt and pepper and cover. Simmer for 10 minutes. Add the beans. Mix the flour and water until smooth, then stir into the bean mixture. Cook until thickened. Let stand for 1 hour to blend flavors, then reheat.

Mrs. M. W. Kurtz, Rosenberg, Texas

BEAN AND STEAK STIR-FRY

1 lb. round steak	1 tsp. salt
2 tbsp. salad oil	1/2 tsp. hot sauce
2 c. green beans, cut	2 med. tomatoes, cut in wedges
diagonally	2 tbsp. soy sauce
4 scallions, sliced	

Cut the steak across grain into paper-thin slices. Heat the oil in a heavy skillet. Add the beans and scallions and sprinkle with salt. Cook, stirring or shaking the skillet, until crisp-tender. Add the steak and cook, stirring, for 3 minutes. Sprinkle hot sauce over all. Add the tomatoes and soy sauce and stir. Cover and cook for 3 minutes longer. One cup sliced cherry tomatoes may be substituted for tomato wedges, if desired. 4 servings.

Top: Green Bean Casserole (page 112)
Bottom: Bean and Steak Stir-Fry (above)

DEEP SOUTH RED BEANS AND RICE

1/2 lb. sliced bacon	1 sm. bay leaf
1 c. minced onions	2 c. cooked rice
1 1-lb. 1-oz. can red beans	

Dice the bacon and cook in a saucepan until light brown. Pour off the fat. Add the onions and cook until bacon is brown. Add the red beans and bay leaf and cover. Simmer for 30 minutes, adding water, if needed and stirring occasionally. Stir in the rice and cover. Cook until rice is heated through. 5-6 servings.

Catherine Tatum, Marianna, Arkansas

BEETS PIQUANT

6 med. cooked beets	1 tbsp. sugar
2 tbsp. butter or margarine	1/2 tsp. salt
2 tbsp. lemon juice	2 tbsp. chopped parsley

Remove skins from the beets and cut beets in thin strips. Melt the butter in a skillet and add the beets. Sprinkle with lemon juice, sugar and salt and cover. Cook over low heat for 10 minutes or until heated through. Sprinkle with parsley. 4 servings.

Ernestina Garcia, Del Rio, Texas

BROCCOLI WITH FRENCH SAUCE

2 lb. fresh broccoli	1 c. chicken bouillon
2 tbsp. butter or margarine	1/2 tsp. Worcestershire sauce
2 tbsp. flour	1/2 c. sliced stuffed olives
1/4 tsp. salt	4 hard-cooked eggs, sliced
Dash of pepper	

Cook the broccoli in boiling, salted water until tender, then drain. Place in a serving dish. Melt the butter in a saucepan and blend in flour, salt and pepper. Stir in the bouillon gradually and cook, stirring, until thick. Add the Worcestershire sauce, olives and eggs and pour over the broccoli. 6 servings.

Grace L. Hollen, Dayton, Virginia

BRUSSELS SPROUTS AU GRATIN

1 lge. package frozen Brussels sprouts	1/2 c. milk
	3 drops of hot sauce
1 sm. green pepper, chopped	1 tsp. Worcestershire sauce
1 1/2 c. chopped celery	Salt and pepper to taste
1 tbsp. butter or margarine	1/2 c. bread crumbs
1/2 c. Cheddar cheese soup	

Cook the Brussels sprouts, covered, in 1-inch boiling, salted water for 7 to 8 minutes, then drain. Place in a greased casserole. Saute the green pepper and celery in butter in a saucepan for 5 minutes. Blend the soup with milk and seasonings and add to green pepper mixture. Bring to boiling point and pour over the Brussels sprouts. Top with crumbs. Bake in a 400-degree oven for 30 minutes. 4-6 servings.

Mrs. Harold Taylor, Laurel, Mississippi

FRENCH RED CABBAGE WITH MARRONS

1 1/2 lb. chestnuts	Salt and pepper to taste
Salad oil	1/2 c. butter
1 lge. red cabbage	1/2 lb. fried sliced bacon,
2 c. dry red wine	crumbled
1 c. water	

Slit sides of chestnut shells. Place in a large, shallow pan and sprinkle with oil. Bake in 450-degree oven for 20 minutes. Remove shells and skin with a sharp-pointed knife. Cut the cabbage into 1/2-inch slices and place in a large casserole. Add the wine and water and season with salt and pepper. Cover. Bake in 325-degree oven for 1 hour. Remove cover. Add the chestnuts and bake for 1 hour longer or until chestnuts are tender and liquid is absorbed. Add the butter and mix well. Place the bacon on top. 6 servings.

Charlotte McCord, Richmond, Virginia

PUREED PARSLEY-CARROTS

3 tbsp. butter or margarine	1 1/2 tsp. salt
1/2 c. chopped fresh onion	1/8 tsp. pepper
4 c. sliced pared carrots	2 tbsp. chopped fresh
1/2 c. milk	parsley

Melt the butter in a saucepan. Add the onion and carrots and cover. Cook over low heat for 30 to 40 minutes or until tender. Puree in an electric blender or food mill, then turn into a saucepan. Add the milk, salt, pepper and parsley and heat through. Place in a serving bowl and garnish with additional parsley. 4 servings.

Pureed Parsley-Carrots (above)

CARROTS A LA BOURGUIGNONNE

2 onions, diced	1/4 c. flour
2 tbsp. butter	1 c. bouillon
12 carrots, sliced lengthwise	Salt and pepper to taste

Saute the onions in butter in a saucepan for 5 minutes. Coat the carrots with flour and add to the onions. Cook until brown. Add the bouillon, salt and pepper and simmer for 30 minutes. 6 servings.

Kathryn Elwert, Wichita Falls, Texas

CAULIFLOWER A LA CURRY

Butter	1/4 tsp. curry powder
2 tbsp. flour	1 cauliflower
1 c. milk	12 to 15 soda crackers,
1/4 lb. Velveeta cheese	crumbled

Melt 2 tablespoons butter in a saucepan and blend in flour. Add the milk slowly and cook until thickened, stirring constantly. Add the cheese and stir until melted. Add the curry powder and remove from heat. Separate the cauliflower into flowerets and cook in boiling, salted water until tender. Drain. Place alternate layers of cauliflower, cheese sauce and cracker crumbs in a greased baking dish and dot with butter. Bake at 350 degrees until lightly browned.

Mrs. Ada B. Dobson, Pascagoula, Mississippi

CREOLE-STYLE CELERY

3 c. celery, cut in 1-in. pieces	3 tbsp. butter
1 1-lb. can tomatoes	2 tbsp. minced green pepper
1 tsp. salt	2 tbsp. minced onion

Place the celery, tomatoes and salt in a saucepan and cover. Cook over low heat until celery is tender. Melt the butter in a saucepan. Add the green pepper and onion and cook until brown. Add the celery mixture and stir well. Cook until liquid has evaporated. 6 servings.

Mrs. Bob Weldon, Kinston, North Carolina

CREOLE CORN CASSEROLE

1 med. onion, chopped	2 hard-cooked eggs, finely chopped
1 green pepper, chopped	1 tsp. Worcestershire sauce
1/2 c. margarine	1/2 tsp. hot sauce
4 tbsp. flour	1 1/2 tsp. salt
2 c. cooked rice	3/4 c. grated cheese
2 c. whole kernel corn	
2 c. mashed canned tomatoes	

Cook the onion and green pepper in margarine in a saucepan until light brown. Add the flour and cook until brown. Add remaining ingredients except cheese and mix well. Pour into a greased casserole and cover with cheese. Bake at 350 degrees until heated through. 6-8 servings.

Mrs. Louise Simpson, Alexander City, Alabama

CORN FRITTERS

1 c. sifted flour	1/2 c. milk
1 tbsp. sugar	Salad oil
1/2 tsp. salt	1 1/2 c. cooked whole kernel
1 tsp. baking powder	corn
1 egg	

Combine the flour, sugar, salt and baking powder in a bowl. Beat the egg with milk and add 1 tablespoon oil and the corn. Stir into the flour mixture until just mixed. Drop from tablespoon into deep oil at 365 degrees and cook for about 4 minutes or until brown. Drain on paper towels. 12-14 fritters.

Mrs. Helen B. Cuppet, El Paso, Texas

FRIED CORN

4 lge. ears of corn	1 tsp. salt
4 slices bacon	1 tbsp. cornstarch
1 tbsp. sugar	

Cut the tips from corn kernels with a sharp knife, then scrape remaining corn from cobs. Cook the bacon in a large skillet over low heat until crisp. Drain and break into large pieces. Drain all except 2 tablespoons bacon drippings from the skillet, then stir in the corn, 1 1/4 cups water, sugar and salt. Bring to a boil and reduce heat. Cover and simmer for 20 to 25 minutes, stirring occasionally. Mix the cornstarch and 2 tablespoons water until smooth and stir into the corn. Bring to a boil and cook for 1 minute. Add the bacon and mix well. 4 servings.

Mrs. Glenn H. Harrison, Plainview, Texas

AUBERGINE-CREVETTE CREOLE

2 sm. eggplant	1/2 bay leaf
1 lge. onion, chopped	1/3 tsp. thyme
1 green pepper, chopped	1 1/2 lb. shrimp, cleaned
1 c. water	1 c. bread crumbs
1 tsp. salt	

Peel and dice the eggplant and cook in boiling water for 10 minutes. Drain and place in a baking dish. Saute the onion and green pepper in small amount of fat in a saucepan until tender. Add the water, salt, bay leaf, thyme and shrimp. Cook for 15 minutes, then stir in bread crumbs. Remove bay leaf and mix shrimp mixture with the eggplant. Bake at 350 degrees for 30 minutes. 6 servings.

Mrs. B. W. Causey, Baton Rouge, Louisiana

Stuffed Eggplant (below)
Stuffed Green Peppers (below)

STUFFED EGGPLANT

2 med. eggplant
1/4 c. oil
1 1/2 lb. ground beef
1/4 c. chopped onion
1/4 c. chopped green
   pepper (opt.)

1/4 clove of garlic, chopped
1 1/4 tsp. hot sauce
1 tsp. salt
1 1/2 c. cooked rice
1 tsp. lemon juice

Slice the eggplant in half. Scoop out some of the pulp and chop. Heat the oil in a skillet. Add the chopped eggplant, beef, onion, green pepper, garlic, hot sauce and salt and saute until eggplant is lightly browned. Add the rice and mix well. Stuff eggplant halves with rice mixture and place, skin side down, in a greased baking dish. Bake in 375-degree oven for 30 minutes. Remove from oven and sprinkle with lemon juice. 4 servings.

STUFFED GREEN PEPPERS

4 med. green peppers
1 1/2 lb. ground beef
1/4 c. chopped onion
1/4 c. chopped green pepper

1 1/4 tsp. hot sauce
1 tsp. salt
1 1/2 c. cooked rice

Remove top of each green pepper and remove white membrane and seeds from inside. Simmer green peppers in boiling water for 15 minutes, then drain. Combine the beef, onion, chopped green pepper, hot sauce and salt in a skillet and saute until green pepper is tender. Add the rice and mix well. Stuff each green pepper with about 3/4 cup rice mixture and place, standing, in a greased baking dish. Bake in 375-degree oven for 30 minutes or until green peppers are tender. Serve hot or cold. 4 servings.

VEGETABLE-STUFFED GREEN PEPPERS

6 med. green peppers
1 c. canned tomatoes
4 tbsp. finely chopped celery
1 1/2 c. canned whole kernel
   corn
1 tbsp. chopped onion

2 tbsp. melted butter
2 eggs, beaten
1/8 tsp. pepper
1/2 c. soft bread crumbs
1 tsp. salt

Wash the green peppers and remove tops and seeds. Reserve tops. Cook the green peppers and reserved tops in boiling, salted water for 4 to 5 minutes and drain. Combine remaining ingredients and place in green peppers. Replace tops. Place in a greased casserole and add small amount of water. Cover. Bake at 350 degrees for 1 hour.

Mrs. Kenneth Norris, Hobbs, New Mexico

LYE HOMINY

5 qt. white corn
1/2 c. lye

6 qt. water

Mix all ingredients in a stone jar or enamel pan and soak for 15 hours or until husks will come off easily. Drain, then wash in cold water several times, removing husks. Place in a kettle and cover with water. Bring to a boil, then simmer until tender, changing water 2 or 3 times. Pack in freezer containers and freeze.

Eula Barker, Faubush, Kentucky

WILTED LEAF LETTUCE

2 lge. bundles leaf lettuce
1/2 tsp. salt or garlic salt
Pepper to taste
2 tsp. sugar (opt.)
3 green onions, chopped

4 slices bacon, chopped
2 to 4 tbsp. vinegar
2 tbsp. water
1 hard-cooked egg, chopped

Shred the lettuce into a bowl and add the salt, pepper, sugar and onions. Fry the bacon in a skillet until crisp and add the vinegar and water. Bring to a boil and pour over the lettuce mixture. Toss until mixed. Sprinkle egg over top. 6 servings.

Lillian Y. Wynn, Sicily Island, Louisiana

FRENCH-FRIED ONIONS

1/2 lb. onions, sliced
1 c. flour
1/2 tsp. salt

1/4 tsp. baking powder
1 egg
1/2 c. milk

Separate the onion slices into rings. Mix the flour, salt and baking powder in a bowl. Add the egg and milk and blend well. Dip the onion rings into batter. Fry in deep hot fat for 2 minutes or until brown. 4-6 servings.

Mrs. Shirley Ann Beddie, Calvin, Louisiana

GLAZED ONIONS

2 lb. small onions
1/2 c. melted butter

6 tbsp. sugar
Paprika

Cook the onions in a large amount of boiling, salted water for about 40 minutes or until tender, then drain. Heat the butter in a skillet. Add the onions and sprinkle with sugar. Cook over low heat for 10 minutes or until onions are glazed, stirring frequently. Sprinkle with paprika. 6 servings.

Mrs. Helen Redmon, Greensboro, North Carolina

STUFFED ONIONS

6 lge. white onions
1 lge. green pepper, chopped
1 lb. ground beef
1/2 tsp. garlic salt

Salt and pepper to taste
1 c. grated Cheddar cheese
1 c. tomato sauce

Cook the onions in boiling, salted water for 45 minutes, then drain. Remove centers of onions carefully and chop centers. Cook the green pepper, ground beef and seasonings in a skillet until beef is brown. Place the onion shells in a casserole and stuff with beef mixture. Top with cheese and tomato sauce. Bake at 350 degrees for 45 minutes.

Mrs. W. S. Youngblood, Altus, Oklahoma

MUSHROOM PAPRIKASH

1 lb. fresh mushrooms
2 tbsp. butter or margarine
1 tsp. fresh lemon juice
2 tbsp. instant minced onion
1 tsp. flour

1/2 tsp. salt
1 tsp. paprika
1/16 tsp. ground red pepper
1/4 c. sour cream

Mushroom Paprikash (above)

Wash and slice the mushrooms. Saute in the butter and lemon juice in a saucepan for 5 to 6 minutes or until mushrooms are tender. Combine the onion, flour, salt, paprika and red pepper and add to the mushrooms. Cook, stirring, for 1 minute. Add the sour cream and heat through. Do not boil. 6 servings.

MUSHROOMS VINAIGRETTE

1/4 c. vinegar	Pepper to taste
1 clove of garlic, halved	3 tbsp. olive oil
2 tbsp. lemon juice	1 tbsp. catsup
1 sm. bay leaf	1 4-oz. can mushroom caps
1/4 tsp. salt	

Combine the vinegar, garlic, lemon juice, bay leaf, salt and pepper in a saucepan and boil for 15 minutes. Cool and add the olive oil and catsup. Drain the mushrooms and place in a bowl. Pour the vinegar mixture over the mushrooms and cover. Refrigerate for at least 12 hours.

Mrs. Peter Smith, Johnson City, Tennessee

STUFFED MIRLITONS

4 lge. mirlitons	1 c. cooked chopped shrimp
1/2 c. diced onion	1 c. bread crumbs
1/4 c. chopped celery	1 1/2 tsp. seasoned salt
3 tbsp. cooking oil	1/8 tsp. cayenne pepper

Halve the mirlitons lengthwise and remove seeds. Cook in boiling, salted water until tender. Scoop out pulp and reserve shells. Mash the pulp. Saute onion and celery in oil in a 10-inch skillet until tender, then stir in the mashed pulp, shrimp, 1/2 cup bread crumbs, seasoned salt and cayenne pepper. Place in reserved shells and cover with remaining crumbs. Place in a baking pan. Bake at 350 degrees for 30 minutes or until brown. 8 servings.

Mrs. Margaret A. McBride, Livingston, Louisiana

OKRA CREOLE

1/4 c. chopped onion	3/4 c. chopped tomatoes
1 sm. green pepper, chopped	1 c. canned whole kernel corn
3 tbsp. bacon drippings	1 tsp. salt
2 c. sliced okra	1/8 tsp. pepper

Cook the onion and green pepper in bacon drippings in a saucepan until onion is golden, stirring frequently. Add the okra and cook for 5 minutes, stirring occasionally. Add remaining ingredients and cover. Simmer for 15 to 20 minutes. 4 servings.

Mrs. Eloise Howerton, Knoxville, Tennessee

HOPPING JOHN

4 c. field peas	Salt to taste
1 ham hock	1 c. packaged precooked rice

Place the peas and ham hock in a large saucepan and cover with water. Add the salt and stir. Bring to a boil and reduce heat. Simmer for about 1 hour and 30 minutes, adding enough boiling water to keep peas covered. Remove the ham hock. Add the rice and stir well. Bring to a boil, then remove from heat. Cover and let stand for 15 minutes. Cut the ham from ham hock and stir into rice mixture.

Mrs. Louis Salter, Columbia, South Carolina

PARSLEYED POTATOES

4 c. small new potatoes	1 c. evaporated milk
1 tsp. savory salt	1 tbsp. grated onion
2 c. boiling water	1/2 c. finely chopped parsley
3 tbsp. margarine	Pepper to taste
3 tbsp. flour	

Scrape the potatoes and place in a saucepan. Add the salt and water and cover. Cook, until tender, then remove from heat. Drain. Melt the margarine in a saucepan and stir in flour. Add the milk and cook, stirring, until thick. Add the potatoes and onion and heat through. Add the parsley and pepper and mix. 6 servings.

Mrs. James Burch, Hughes, Arkansas

POTATO PUFFS

1 c. sifted flour	1 c. mashed potatoes
1/2 tbsp. salt	2 eggs
1 tbsp. baking powder	3/4 c. milk

Sift the flour, salt and baking powder together into a bowl and add the potatoes. Add the eggs and milk and beat well. Drop by tablespoonfuls into deep, hot fat and fry until puffed and browned. Serve hot.

Mrs. Hal Jones, Dandridge, Tennessee

SPINACH DELICIOUS

1 14-oz. package frozen chopped spinach	2 tbsp. horseradish
2 tbsp. butter or margarine	1/2 tsp. salt
1/4 c. light cream	1/8 tsp. pepper

Prepare the spinach according to package directions and drain. Place in a saucepan. Add remaining ingredients and heat through. Garnish with hard-cooked egg slices. One pound fresh spinach, cooked, may be substituted for frozen spinach. 4 servings.

Shirley L. Drewry, Wilmington, Delaware

SQUASH SOUFFLE

1 tbsp. butter	1/2 c. milk
1 tbsp. flour	3 egg yolks, beaten
1/8 tsp. salt	1 c. cooked squash
1/8 tsp. pepper	2 egg whites, stiffly beaten

Melt the butter in a saucepan and stir in flour, salt and pepper. Remove from heat and add milk gradually. Cook over low heat for 3 minutes, stirring constantly. Stir into the egg yolks slowly. Stir in the squash and fold in the egg whites. Turn into a casserole. Bake at 325 degrees for 30 to 35 minutes.

Mrs. Bill Walker, Statesville, North Carolina

ZUCCHINI IN SKILLET

4 med. zucchini	1 tsp. salt
2 fresh tomatoes	1/2 tsp. crushed basil
2 tbsp. corn oil	1/4 tsp. pepper
1 sm. onion, sliced	1 bay leaf
1 tbsp. chopped pimento	

Cut the zucchini into 1-inch slices. Peel and chop the tomatoes. Heat the corn oil in a skillet. Add the onion and saute until lightly browned. Add the zucchini, tomatoes, pimento, salt, basil, pepper and bay leaf. Cover and simmer for about 25 minutes or until zucchini is tender. Remove the bay leaf. 4-6 servings.

Zucchini in Skillet (above)

STUFFED ZUCCHINI

6 med. zucchini	1 clove of garlic, minced
1/2 lb. ground beef	3/4 tsp. salt
1 slice bacon, chopped	1/8 tsp. pepper
1/2 c. minced parsley	1/4 c. salad oil
1/2 c. finely chopped tomatoes	2 slices bread
1/2 c. finely chopped onion	1/4 c. milk

Cut the zucchini in half lengthwise and scoop out pulp, leaving 1/4-inch shells. Dice the pulp and reserve shells. Brown the beef and bacon in a large skillet. Add the diced squash, parsley, tomatoes, onion, garlic, salt, pepper and oil and cook, stirring, for 5 minutes. Soak the bread in the milk for several minutes, then squeeze dry. Add to the squash mixture and mix well. Spoon into reserved shells and place side by side in the skillet. Add about 1 cup water and cover. Cook over low heat for 10 minutes or until squash shell is tender.

Mrs. Roy Davis, Troutman, North Carolina

CANDIED SWEET POTATOES

6 med. sweet potatoes	2 tbsp. butter
Salt	1 lemon, sliced (opt.)
1 c. sugar	

Cook the sweet potatoes in boiling, salted water for 15 minutes. Drain and cool. Peel and slice. Place in a greased baking dish. Mix the sugar, butter and 1/2 cup water in a saucepan and cook for 3 minutes. Pour over the potatoes and place lemon slices on top. Bake at 300 degrees for 30 minutes or until brown, basting occasionally.

Mrs. Bennie Hubbard, Centreville, Alabama

LOUISIANA YAM-APRICOT PUDDING

2/3 c. water	2 tsp. grated lemon peel
1/3 c. butter or margarine	4 tsp. lemon juice
1/3 c. (firmly packed) light	3 tbsp. apricot liqueur
brown sugar	3/4 c. diced dried apricots
6 med. Louisiana yams, cooked	1 c. heavy cream
1/4 tsp. salt	2 tbsp. sugar

Bring the water to a boil in a large saucepan. Add the butter and brown sugar and stir until smooth. Peel and mash the yams and blend into the butter mixture. Add the salt, 1 teaspoon lemon peel, lemon juice, liqueur and apricots and turn into a greased 1-quart baking dish. Bake in 350-degree oven for 30 minutes. Whip the cream, sugar and remaining lemon peel in a bowl until soft peaks form. Serve with the yam mixture. Three 16-ounce cans Louisiana yams, drained and mashed, may be substituted for the fresh yams. 8-10 servings.

Photograph for this recipe on page 110.

BAKED TOMATO CUPS

3/4 c. bread crumbs
2 tbsp. butter
6 med. tomatoes
1/2 tsp. salt

Pepper to taste
1 c. canned whole kernel corn
3/4 c. canned mushrooms

Saute the bread crumbs in butter in a saucepan until brown. Cut thin slices from stem ends of tomatoes and remove pulp. Reserve 1 cup pulp. Combine the salt, pepper, corn, mushrooms, reserved tomato pulp and 1/2 cup buttered crumbs. Fill tomatoes with corn mixture and sprinkle with remaining crumbs. Place in a baking dish. Bake at 350 degrees for 30 minutes.

Mrs. Ella Jo Adams, Allen, Texas

FRIED GREEN TOMATOES

6 med. green tomatoes
1 egg, slightly beaten
1/2 tsp. salt

Dash of pepper
1/2 c. fine dry bread crumbs

Slice the tomatoes 1/2 inch thick. Mix the egg with salt and pepper. Dip tomato slices into crumbs, then in egg. Dip in crumbs again. Fry in a small amount of fat in a skillet until browned on both sides.

Mrs. S. E. Adams, Hays, North Carolina

TOMATOES VINAIGRETTE

1 lge. Spanish onion
2 lge. tomatoes, thinly sliced
1 lge. cucumber, thinly sliced
2 tbsp. chopped parsley
1/2 c. salad oil
1/4 tsp. salt
1/4 c. wine vinegar

1/2 tsp. garlic salt
1/4 tsp. ground savory
1/4 tsp. celery salt
1/4 tsp. crumbled tarragon
1/4 tsp. pepper
1/2 tsp. crumbled bay leaf

Cut the onion into thin slices and separate into rings. Layer the tomatoes, cucumber, parsley and onion rings in a shallow dish. Blend remaining ingredients and pour over vegetables. Cover and chill overnight. Drain, then serve in individual dishes. 4-5 servings.

Mary Elizabeth Kloos, Panama City, Florida

TURNIPS

1/4 lb. salt pork
4 c. sliced turnips
Pepper to taste

1 tbsp. sugar
1/2 c. cornmeal

Wash the pork and cut into cubes. Cook in 2 quarts boiling, salted water until tender. Add the turnips and simmer until tender. Stir in the pepper, sugar and cornmeal and cook for 1 minute longer.

Mrs. Harris Newman, Estill Springs, Tennessee

Ripe Olive Polenta (page 137)

creole egg, cheese, and cereal dishes

Much of the life of a Creole family revolved around the church. And an important part of that church life was the Lenten season — the six weeks following Mardi Gras when light and often meatless meals were the rule. For such days, creative Creole homemakers turned to eggs, cheese, and cereals and developed some of the most un-usual and delicious dishes in the entire Creole repertoire.

Never-Fail Fluffy Omelet is one example of these dishes. It is economical, meatless, and so easy to prepare that you will come to depend on it whenever you need a meal in a hurry. Versatile omelets are excellent at breakfast, lunch, or dinner! Bacon Quiche Lorraine is a pie-like blend of eggs, bacon, and pastry that originated in France but is featured in this recipe with uniquely Creole season-ings. Cottage Rice with Shrimp Sauce . . . Rice Jamba-laya . . . Cheese Fondue . . . Scrambled Eggs and Mushrooms . . . these are just some of the wonderfully economical recipes awaiting you in these pages.

As you begin to browse, you'll discover that omelets and souffles can be appetite-appealing ways to use up bits of leftover meat and vegetables . . . that scrambled eggs may be more than just a breakfast dish . . . and that rice and grits have infinite possibilities on your menus. In short, you'll discover, as generations of Creole homemakers did, that cheese, eggs, and cereals can bring variety and econ-omy to your menu — at any time of the year!

Spanish Vegetable Omelet (below)

SPANISH VEGETABLE OMELET

2 sm. tomatoes
Olive oil
Butter or margarine
1/2 c. finely chopped onion
1 med. green pepper, chopped
1/4 c. chopped pimento-
    stuffed olives

1 tbsp. chopped parsley
1/2 tsp. salt
8 eggs, beaten
Sm. whole pimento-stuffed
    olives
Watercress

Peel, seed and dice the tomatoes. Heat 1 tablespoon olive oil and 1 tablespoon butter in a 10-inch omelet pan. Add the onion and cook until tender. Add small amount of olive oil, if necessary. Add the green pepper and tomatoes and cook, stirring occasionally, until green pepper is tender. Remove from pan with a slotted spoon and discard any liquid in pan. Stir the vegetable mixture, chopped olives, parsley and salt into the eggs. Wipe pan dry with paper towels. Heat 1 tablespoon butter in the pan. Add the egg mixture and cook over low heat, running a spatula around edges occasionally to allow uncooked egg to go to bottom, until omelet is almost firm. Loosen around edges and invert a plate over top of the pan. Turn omelet out onto the plate. Clean pan with paper towels and add small amount of butter. Discard any liquid from omelet. Slide omelet back into pan. Cook over low heat until lightly browned and invert onto serving plate in same manner as before. Garnish with whole olives and watercress.

SCRAMBLED EGGS AND MUSHROOMS

1 sm. can mushroom stems and
    pieces

1 sm. onion, chopped
4 eggs

Drain the mushroom liquid into a skillet. Add the onion and simmer until onion is tender and liquid is evaporated. Whip the eggs in a bowl until frothy. Add the mushrooms to onion and stir. Add the eggs and cook, stirring constantly, until eggs are set.

Mrs. Naomi Burrows, Fort Lauderdale, Florida

MUSHROOMS AND EGGS A LA RITZ

1/4 lb. fresh mushrooms	1 1/2 c. light cream or milk
6 tbsp. butter or margarine	6 hard-cooked eggs
1 tbsp. finely chopped onion	4 tsp. dry sherry
3 tbsp. flour	1 10-oz. package frozen
3/4 tsp. salt	patty shells
1/16 tsp. ground red pepper	

Rinse, pat dry and slice the mushrooms. Heat 2 tablespoons butter in a small skillet. Add the mushrooms and onion and saute for 4 to 5 minutes. Heat remaining butter in a medium saucepan. Remove from heat and stir in the flour, salt and red pepper until smooth. Stir in the cream gradually and return to heat. Bring to boiling point and cook until thickened and smooth, stirring constantly. Dice 5 eggs and stir into the cream sauce. Stir in the mushrooms, onion and sherry and heat through. Do not boil. Bake the patty shells according to package directions and spoon the mushroom mixture into each shell. Slice remaining egg into 6 wedges and place 1 wedge on mushroom mixture in each shell. Garnish each with sprig of parsley, if desired. One 3 to 4-ounce can sliced mushrooms, drained, may be substituted for fresh mushrooms.

Mushrooms and Eggs a la Ritz (above)

AVOCADO OMELET

1 lge. ripe avocado	6 eggs
Salt	2 tbsp. water
Pepper to taste	2 tbsp. margarine
1/4 tsp. cayenne pepper	

Pare the avocado and cut in strips. Sprinkle with 1/2 teaspoon salt, pepper and cayenne pepper. Place the eggs, water, salt to taste and pepper in a bowl and beat until light and fluffy. Melt the margarine in a frying pan. Add the avocado and stir until coated with margarine. Increase heat and cook until margarine is light brown. Add the eggs and cook, lifting eggs around edge with a spatula to let uncooked portion run underneath, until done. Garnish with red pepper strips.

Photograph for this recipe on page 5.

CURRIED EGGS WITH SHRIMP AND CHEESE

1 doz. hard-boiled eggs	1 lb. cooked cleaned shrimp
Mayonnaise	1/4 c. dry sherry
Salt and mustard to taste	1/2 tsp. curry powder
Hot sauce to taste	2 cans cheese soup
1/4 lb. grated sharp cheese	

Cut the eggs in half lengthwise. Mix the egg yolks with enough mayonnaise to moisten, salt, mustard and hot sauce. Stuff the egg whites with yolk mixture and place in a shallow casserole. Mix the cheese, shrimp, sherry, curry powder and soup well and pour over eggs. Bake in 350-degree oven for about 30 minutes or until bubbly.

Mrs. Winston Broadfoot, Chapel Hill, North Carolina

SCRAMBLED EGGS AND RICE

4 eggs	Salt and pepper to taste
3 c. cooked rice	2 tbsp. butter

Beat the eggs in a bowl well and stir in the rice, salt and pepper. Melt the butter in a frying pan. Add the egg mixture and cook over low heat, stirring constantly, until eggs are set.

Mrs. M. L. Baggette, Daphne, Alabama

SHIRRED EGGS AND HAM

6 slices boiled ham	Salt and pepper to taste
Light cream	6 tbsp. grated Cheddar cheese
12 eggs	

Line each of 6 ramekins or individual casseroles with a boiled ham slice and pour 3 tablespoons cream into each ramekin. Break the eggs into a small bowl, one at a time, and place 2 eggs in each ramekin, being careful not to break the yolks. Sprinkle each ramekin with salt, pepper and 1 tablespoon cheese and cover with foil. Bake in 325-degree oven for 20 to 25 minutes or until eggs are set.

Mrs. Mary Cooper, Dover, Delaware

CREOLEAN OMELETTE

3 lge. tomatoes	1/4 c. chili sauce
1 onion	5 lge. stuffed olives, sliced
1 green pepper	1 tbsp. cornstarch
4 tbsp. margarine	5 tbsp. water
1 clove of garlic, crushed	6 eggs, separated
1 tsp. salt	1/4 tsp. paprika
1/4 tsp. cayenne pepper	

Scald, skin and chop the tomatoes. Peel and slice the onion. Seed and chop the green pepper. Melt 2 tablespoons margarine in a saucepan. Add the tomatoes, green pepper, onion, garlic, 1/2 teaspoon salt, cayenne pepper, chili sauce and olives and bring to a boil. Reduce heat and simmer for 15 minutes, stirring occasionally. Mix the cornstarch and 2 tablespoons water and stir into the tomato mixture. Cook until thickened. Beat the egg yolks, paprika and remaining salt and water in a bowl until thick and lemon colored. Beat the egg whites in a bowl until stiff peaks form, then fold in the egg yolk mixture. Melt remaining margarine in a large skillet over low heat. Add the egg mixture and cook until light brown. Fold over. Bake at 350 degrees until center is set. Place on a platter and pour the sauce over the omelet. Serve immediately. One can tomatoes may be substituted for fresh tomatoes. 4 servings.

Creolean Omelette (above)

NEVER-FAIL FLUFFY OMELET

2 tbsp. quick-cooking tapioca
3/4 tsp. salt
1/8 tsp. pepper
3/4 c. milk
1 tbsp. butter
4 eggs, separated

Combine the tapioca, salt, pepper and milk in a saucepan. Place over low heat and cook until mixture comes to a boil, stirring constantly. Add the butter and remove from heat. Cool slightly. Beat the egg yolks in a bowl until thick and lemon colored. Stir in milk mixture slowly and mix well. Fold into stiffly beaten egg whites. Turn into a hot, greased 10-inch skillet. Cook over low heat for 3 minutes. Bake at 350 degrees for 15 minutes or until knife inserted in center comes out clean. Cut across center of omelet not quite to bottom and fold over. Place on a hot platter.

Mrs. David Fisher, Newport News, Virginia

BACON QUICHE LORRAINE

1 unbaked 8-in. pie shell
4 slices bacon
1 med. onion, sliced
3/4 c. milk
2 eggs, beaten
1/2 c. grated Cheddar cheese
1/2 tsp. salt
1/4 tsp. pepper
2 tbsp. chopped parsley
Pinch of sugar and nutmeg
(opt.)
Dash of red pepper (opt.)
Paprika to taste

Chill the pie shell or place in freezer for 5 minutes. Fry the bacon in a skillet until crisp, then drain. Cook the onion in bacon fat in the skillet until transparent. Combine the milk, eggs, 1/4 cup cheese, salt, pepper, parsley, sugar, nutmeg and red pepper in a bowl. Add the bacon and onion and pour into the pie shell. Sprinkle with remaining cheese and sprinkle with paprika. Bake at 350 degrees for 25 to 35 minutes or until firm.

Lamartha McCaine, Toccoa, Georgia

CHEESE-CELERY CASSEROLE

1 med. bunch celery
1/2 lb. Cheddar cheese, grated
3 hard-cooked eggs, sliced
1 tsp. salt
Dash of hot sauce
1/2 c. blanched slivered
almonds
2 c. white sauce
1 c. bread crumbs
Butter

Cut the celery in 1-inch pieces and cook in boiling, salted water until tender. Drain. Place alternate layers of celery, cheese and eggs in a greased casserole. Add the salt, hot sauce and almonds. Cover with white sauce, then bread crumbs and dot with butter. Bake at 350 degrees for about 30 minutes or until brown and bubbly. 6 servings.

Mrs. Harvyl Boaz, Paducah, Kentucky

BASQUE PIPERADE

1 onion
1 clove of garlic, crushed
1 green pepper
5 med. tomatoes
1 tsp. salt
1 tsp. dried basil

Pepper to taste
1/8 lb. sliced ham, cut in
   strips
6 eggs
3 tbsp. margarine

Peel and chop the onion. Saute the onion and garlic in 1 tablespoon fat in a saucepan over low heat until soft. Seed the green pepper. Slice several rings from 1 end and reserve. Cut remaining green pepper into strips and add to the onion mixture. Scald and skin the tomatoes and chop 4 tomatoes fine. Stir into onion mixture and cook, stirring, for several minutes. Season with 1/2 teaspoon salt, basil and pepper and cook until most of the liquid has evaporated. Keep hot. Fry the ham in a skillet until heated through and remove from skillet. Beat the eggs, 2 tablespoons water and remaining salt in a bowl until light and fluffy. Melt the margarine in the skillet over low heat. Add the egg mixture and cook until bottom is just set. Add the ham and tomato mixture and cook to desired doneness, stirring carefully and leaving bottom layer intact. Slice remaining tomato and place on the omelet. Garnish with reserved green pepper rings.

Basque Piperade (above)

133

SPINACH CASSEROLE

1 10-oz. package frozen chopped spinach	1/8 tsp. pepper
3 tbsp. margarine	1 c. milk
3 tbsp. cornstarch	4 eggs, separated
1/2 tsp. salt	1/4 tsp. ground nutmeg
	Spicy Tomato Sauce

Cook the spinach according to package directions, then drain well. Melt the margarine in a small, heavy saucepan over medium heat, then stir in the cornstarch, salt and pepper until smooth. Remove from heat. Stir in the milk gradually and cook over medium heat, stirring constantly, until mixture comes to a boil. Cook, stirring, for 1 minute. Remove from heat. Beat the egg yolks slightly, then stir into hot mixture gradually. Stir in the spinach and nutmeg and mix well. Beat the egg whites until stiff peaks form and fold into the spinach mixture. Spoon into a 1 1/2-quart casserole or souffle dish. Bake in 375-degree oven for 30 to 35 minutes or until a knife inserted in center comes out clean. Serve immediately with Spicy Tomato Sauce. 4 servings.

Spicy Tomato Sauce

1 14-oz. can stewed tomatoes	1/4 tsp. salt
1 3-oz. can mushrooms	1/4 tsp. dried basil leaves
2 tbsp. cornstarch	Dash of Worcestershire sauce

Mix the tomatoes, mushrooms, cornstarch, salt, basil and Worcestershire sauce in a small saucepan. Bring to a boil over medium heat, stirring constantly, then cook for 1 minute.

CHEESE FLUFF

4 eggs, separated	1 c. grated cheese
1 c. milk	Salt and pepper to taste
1 c. cracker crumbs	

Beat the egg yolks well in a baking dish, then stir in the milk and cracker crumbs. Beat the egg whites until stiff and fold into the milk mixture. Fold in the cheese, salt and pepper. Place the baking dish in a shallow pan of water. Bake in a 375-degree oven until a knife inserted in the center comes out clean.

Mrs. Bill Morrison, Alexander City, Alabama

CHEESE LOAF DELIGHT

2 tbsp. sugar	1 c. milk
1/2 tsp. salt	1 lb. longhorn cheese, grated
3 egg yolks	1 sm. can pimento strips, drained
1 tbsp. dry mustard	1 c. bread crumbs
1 tbsp. butter	Cracker crumbs
1/2 c. vinegar	

Spinach Casserole (page 134)

Combine sugar, salt, egg yolks, mustard, butter, vinegar and milk in a saucepan and cook until smooth, stirring constantly. Mix the cheese, pimento strips and bread crumbs in a bowl. Add the milk mixture and mix well. Grease a ring mold well and sprinkle with cracker crumbs. Pour the egg mixture into the mold. Bake at 350 degrees for 30 to 40 minutes. Let set for several minutes before removing from mold.

Mrs. Louis Perkins, Flemingsburg, Kentucky

CRAB RAREBIT

1 7-oz. can crab	1 tbsp. lemon juice
2 slices fried bacon, crumbled	1/2 tsp. sugar
1/2 c. chopped onion	1/2 tsp. curry powder
1/2 c. chopped celery	1 clove of garlic, minced
1 can Cheddar cheese soup	Hot sauce to taste
1 1-lb. can tomatoes, drained	

Drain and flake the crab. Cook the bacon, onion and celery in a saucepan until vegetables are tender. Stir in the soup and mix well. Add remaining ingredients except crab and simmer for 45 minutes, stirring occasionally. Add the crab and heat through. 4-6 servings.

Mrs. Rose H. Lavinder, Columbus, Georgia

NEVER-FAIL CHEESE SOUFFLE

1 can mushroom soup
1/2 lb. cheese, grated

6 eggs, separated
1/2 tsp. salt

Pour the soup into top of a double boiler and place over boiling water. Heat through. Add the cheese and stir until cheese is melted. Stir in the beaten egg yolks and cool. Fold in the stiffly beaten egg whites and pour into a greased baking dish. Place in a pan of water. Bake in 350-degree oven for 20 minutes or until done. 4-5 servings.

Mrs. Helen S. Moseley, Ozark, Alabama

CREOLE GRITS

1 c. grits
1 sm. can tomatoes

1/2 c. chopped onions
6 slices crisp bacon, crumbled

Cook the grits according to package directions. Stir in the tomatoes, onions and bacon and place in a casserole. Bake at 400 degrees for about 1 hour.

Mrs. Nell Dorsey, Opp, Alabama

FRIED GRITS

1 qt. milk
1 tsp. salt
1/4 c. margarine
1 c. quick-cooking grits

1 c. grated sharp Cheddar
  cheese
1/4 c. melted margarine

Place the milk, salt and margarine in a saucepan and heat until the margarine melts. Add the grits slowly and cook until thick, stirring frequently. Remove from heat and beat with an electric mixer for 5 minutes. Pour into an 8 x 13-inch pan and chill. Cut into 1 x 2-inch pieces and place in a casserole. Sprinkle with cheese and pour melted margarine over top. Bake at 350 degrees for 40 minutes. 6 servings.

Mrs. W. E. Semands, Houston, Texas

SOUTHERN GRITS DELUXE

1 1/2 c. yellow grits
6 c. boiling water
3/4 c. margarine
1 lb. American cheese, grated

2 tsp. salt
6 drops of hot sauce
4 eggs, well beaten

Stir the grits into the boiling water in a saucepan and cook for 20 minutes, stirring frequently. Stir in remaining ingredients and place in a greased casserole. Bake at 350 degrees for 1 hour.

Mrs. W. E. Frashuer, Robstown, Texas

CREOLE CASSEROLE

1 c. elbow macaroni	1 tsp. Worcestershire sauce
1 can tomatoes with green	1/4 tsp. salt
chilies	Dash of pepper
1 can tomatoes	1/2 lb. American cheese,
1 c. bread crumbs	grated
1 c. diced green pepper	

Cook the macaroni according to package directions, then drain. Stir in remaining ingredients except 1/2 of the cheese and place in a greased casserole. Sprinkle with remaining cheese. Bake at 350 degrees for 30 to 40 minutes.

Mrs. Carl Pickett, Pocahontas, Arkansas

MACARONI SAUTE

1 8-oz. package elbow	1 lb. ground beef (opt.)
macaroni	1 8-oz. can tomato paste
1/2 c. chopped onion	2 1/2 c. water
1/2 c. chopped green pepper	1 tsp. salt
1 clove of garlic, minced	1/4 tsp. pepper
1/2 c. cooking oil	2 tsp. Worcestershire sauce

Saute the macaroni, onion, green pepper and garlic in the oil in a saucepan until macaroni is yellow. Add the beef and cook until the beef is brown. Add remaining ingredients and bring to a boil. Cover and simmer for about 20 minutes, stirring occasionally. 6 servings.

Mrs. Hollis Morgan, Smithville, Mississippi

RIPE OLIVE POLENTA

1 4-oz. can sliced	2 eggs, beaten
mushrooms	1 1/2 c. canned California
1 1/2 c. yellow cornmeal	pitted ripe olives
1 tsp. seasoned salt	1 c. grated Romano cheese
3 c. chicken broth	

Drain the mushrooms and reserve liquid. Add enough water to reserved liquid to make 1 cup liquid. Stir in the cornmeal and seasoned salt. Stir into boiling broth in top of a double boiler and cook over moderate heat, stirring, until thickened. Place over boiling water and cover. Cook for 15 minutes. Stir in eggs slowly until blended. Spoon 1/3 of the mixture into an oiled 1 1/2-quart ovenproof bowl, smoothing to make even. Drain the olives and cut into chunks. Sprinkle half the olives on cornmeal mixture. Sprinkle with 1/3 cup cheese and half the mushrooms. Add half the remaining cornmeal mixture and smooth in even layer. Top with remaining olives, 1/3 cup cheese and remaining mushrooms and cover with remaining cornmeal mixture. Bake at 350 degrees for 20 minutes. Run a spatula around edge of bowl to loosen, then turn out onto a serving plate. Sprinkle remaining cheese over top. 8 servings.

Photograph for this recipe on page 126.

COTTAGE RICE WITH SHRIMP SAUCE

1 4 3/4-oz. package precooked rice	1/2 tsp. pepper
2 tbsp. butter	1 can frozen shrimp soup
1 tsp. instant minced onion	1/4 c. milk
3 eggs, beaten	1 tbsp. dry sherry
2 c. cottage cheese	1 c. cooked cleaned
1 tsp. seasoned salt	shrimp (opt.)

Cook the rice according to package directions, adding the butter and onion. Add the eggs, cottage cheese, salt and pepper and mix well. Pour into a well-greased 9 x 5 x 3-inch loaf pan and place in pan of hot water. Bake in 350-degree oven for 1 hour to 1 hour and 15 minutes or until set. Remove from oven and let stand for 10 minutes. Combine the soup, milk and sherry in a saucepan. Cook, stirring frequently, until heated through. Add the shrimp and mix well. Place the rice mixture in a heated serving dish and pour shrimp mixture over top. 6 servings.

Mrs. James B. Rogers, Demopolis, Alabama

ROASTED RICE

1 c. long grain rice	1/4 c. minced onion
3 bouillon cubes	1 tsp. celery salt
2 1/2 c. boiling water	1/4 c. butter or margarine

Spread the rice in a shallow baking pan. Bake in 375-degree oven for about 15 minutes or until golden brown, stirring occasionally. Place in a 1 1/2-quart casserole. Dissolve the bouillon cubes in the water and stir into the rice. Stir in remaining ingredients and cover. Bake at 350 degrees for 45 minutes. 6 servings.

Mrs. Vida Odom, Ashville, Alabama

RICE JAMBALAYA

1/4 c. butter	1/2 c. diced celery
1 c. rice	3 c. broth or water
1 2-oz. can mushrooms	2 c. stewed tomatoes
1/2 c. chopped onion	1/2 tsp. chili powder
1/2 c. chopped green pepper	2 tsp. salt

Melt the butter in a heavy skillet. Add the rice and cook, stirring constantly, for about 10 minutes or until lightly browned. Add the mushrooms, onion, green pepper and celery and cook until vegetables are tender. Stir in remaining ingredients. Place in a greased casserole and cover. Bake at 350 degrees for 45 minutes. Remove cover and bake for 10 minutes longer. 8 servings.

Mrs. G. A. Hendrix, Little Rock, Arkansas

FRIED RICE

2 tbsp. shortening	1 egg
1 c. cooked cleaned shrimp	2 c. cooked rice
1 sm. onion, diced	1/4 tsp. salt

| 1/2 tsp. monosodium glutamate | 1 green onion, chopped |
| 2 tsp. soy sauce | 1/4 c. shredded lettuce |

Melt the shortening in a large, heavy skillet. Add the shrimp and onion and cook until onion is brown. Add the egg, rice, salt, monosodium glutamate, soy sauce, green onion and lettuce and cook until lettuce is wilted. 4 servings.

Mrs. John Scott, Gulfport, Mississippi

CREOLE SPAGHETTI SPECIAL

3 slices bacon, diced	1 lb. ground pork
5 med. onions, chopped	3 cans tomatoes
2 tbsp. salt	4 tbsp. soy sauce
1 tsp. pepper	2 tsp. basil
3 med. carrots, grated	3 8-oz. packages spaghetti
2 1/2 lb. ground beef	Grated Parmesan cheese

Fry the bacon in a kettle until partially done. Add the onions and cook until onions are tender. Add the salt, pepper and carrots and mix well. Add the beef and pork and cook, stirring, until the beef loses red color. Stir in the tomatoes and liquid, breaking up tomatoes with a spoon, then stir in the soy sauce and basil. Simmer for about 30 minutes or until liquid has evaporated. Cook the spaghetti according to package directions, then drain. Serve with the meat sauce and sprinkle with Parmesan cheese. 18 servings.

Creole Spaghetti Special (above)

creole desserts and beverages

Every Creole cook knew that the beverages accompanying a meal and the dessert that finishes it have much to do with how people enjoy that meal. For this reason, careful attention was paid to the development of beverage and dessert recipes to complement every meal, from the lightest to the richest.

Some of the best, family-approved recipes for desserts and beverages are shared with you now in this section. Some recipes are so traditionally Creole that they are forever part of the cuisine; others can be found throughout the Southland. There's a recipe for Creole Pralines, the rich and sweet, pecan-packed candy so much a part of New Orleans menus . . . Crepes Suzette, the elegant pancake-like dessert featured at elegant dinners everywhere . . . and Ambrosia, the tart fruit dessert no southern holiday meal would be complete without.

You'll also want to try recipes for French Hot Chocolate, a rich beverage that could be an interesting party drink . . . Cafe au Lait, the light, cream-rich coffee so loved in Creole homes . . . and Cafe Brulot, that especially Creole beverage that is served in all its flaming magnificence.

The next time you want a dessert that will finish your meal with a special note, or a beverage to bring compliments from everyone around your table, turn to these pages. You're certain to find a home-tested recipe that you can depend on!

Jam Omelet (below)

JAM OMELET

3 eggs, separated
1 1/2 tsp. sugar
1 1/2 tbsp. light cream

2 tbsp. butter or margarine
3/4 c. strawberry jam, heated
2 tsp. confectioners' sugar

Place the egg yolks, sugar and cream in a bowl and beat until lemon colored. Beat the egg whites in a bowl until stiff peaks form, then fold in the yolk mixture. Melt the butter in a frypan and add the egg mixture. Spread with a spoon, then cover. Cook over very low heat, removing frypan from heat occasionally, if needed, until omelet is cooked through. Spread the jam on half the omelet, then fold remaining omelet over the jam. Sprinkle with confectioners' sugar in square design.

BLACKBERRY JAM CAKE

2/3 c. butter
2 c. sugar
4 eggs, separated
1 c. blackberry jam
3 c. flour

1 tsp. soda
1 tsp. cloves
1 tsp. allspice
1 tsp. cinnamon
1 c. buttermilk

Cream the butter and sugar in a bowl, then add beaten egg yolks and jam. Sift flour, soda and spices together and add to creamed mixture alternately with the milk. Fold in stiffly beaten egg whites and pour into 4 greased and floured 8-inch cake pans. Bake at 350 degrees for 30 to 35 minutes and cool on cake racks. Frost with divinity icing.

Mrs. Iona C. O'Brien, St. Petersburg, Florida

DELICIOUS POUND CAKE

2 sticks butter or margarine	2 c. flour
2 c. sugar	1 tsp. vanilla
5 lge. eggs	1 tsp. lemon extract

Cream the butter with electric mixer for 20 minutes. Add the sugar, 1/2 cup at a time, then beat for 20 minutes. Add the eggs, one at a time. Add the flour, small amount at a time, beating with mixer at low speed. Add the flavorings and pour into a greased tube pan. Bake in 350-degree oven for 1 hour. Reduce temperature to 325 degrees and bake for 10 minutes longer. Cool on rack.

Helen Chandler, New Port Richey, Florida

OLD-FASHIONED GINGERBREAD

1/2 c. butter or shortening	1 1/2 tsp. soda
1/2 c. sugar	1 tsp. cinnamon
1 egg, beaten	1 tsp. ginger
1 c. molasses or cane syrup	1/2 tsp. salt
2 1/2 c. flour	1 c. hot water

Cream the butter and sugar in a bowl and stir in the egg and molasses. Sift dry ingredients together and stir into the sugar mixture. Stir in the hot water and beat until smooth. Pour into a greased 9-inch square pan. Bake at 350 degrees for 35 minutes.

Mrs. Agnes S. Moore, White Castle, Louisiana

SOUR CREAM-CHOCOLATE CAKE

1 1/4 c. sugar	2 tbsp. melted butter
1 3/4 c sifted flour	2 eggs, well beaten
4 tbsp. cocoa	2 tsp. soda
1/4 tsp. salt	4 tbsp. boiling water
1 1/2 c. sour cream	

Mix the sugar, flour, cocoa and salt in a mixing bowl. Add the sour cream, butter and eggs and beat until smooth. Dissolve soda in the water, stir into sour cream mixture and beat well. Pour into greased and floured oblong baking pan. Bake at 350 degrees until cake tests done. Cool and frost with chocolate or Seven-Minute icing.

Minnie M. George, Seiling, Oklahoma

Gateaux Galore (below)

GATEAUX GALORE

5 oz. sweet chocolate	1 1/4 c. confectioners' sugar
2 baked chocolate cake layers	2 tbsp. concentrated orange
Orange candy slices	juice
1/2 c. butter	1/2 tsp. grated orange rind

Melt the chocolate over boiling water and spread over 1 cake layer. Decorate with candy slices while soft. Cool until chocolate hardens. Cream the butter in a bowl. Stir in the sugar gradually and cream well. Add the orange juice and grated rind and stir until smooth. Spread 3/4 of the mixture over remaining cake layer and place the chocolate-covered layer over the butter mixture. Pipe remaining butter mixture onto top layer in spoke design.

FRUITCAKE

1 c. salad oil	1 tsp. cloves
1 1/2 c. (firmly packed) brown	1 c. orange juice
sugar	1 c. thinly sliced citron
4 eggs	1 c. chopped candied pineapple
3 c. sifted all-purpose flour	1 1/2 c. whole candied cherries
1 tsp. baking powder	1 c. seedless raisins
2 tsp. salt	1 c. chopped figs
2 tsp. cinnamon	3 c. chopped nuts
2 tsp. allspice	

Preheat oven to 275 degrees. Combine the oil, sugar and eggs in a mixing bowl and beat with electric mixer for 2 minutes. Sift 2 cups flour with baking powder, salt and spices and stir into oil mixture alternately with orange juice. Mix remaining flour with fruits and nuts, add to egg mixture and mix well. Pour into 2 greased and brown paper-lined 9 x 5 x 3-inch loaf pans. Place a pan of water on lower oven rack. Bake cakes for 2 hours and 30 minutes to 3 hours. Remove from oven and let stand for 15 minutes before removing from pans. Cool thoroughly on racks, then remove paper. Wrap in aluminum foil and store for several weeks to ripen. Cakes may be wrapped in a cloth dampened with brandy or wine, if desired.

Mrs. Ruth Nell Germany, Ashland, Alabama

ROCKS

1 lb. butter, melted	1 lb. seedless raisins
2 1/2 c. sugar	1 c. chopped candied cherries
2 eggs	1 c. chopped candied pineapple
5 c. (about) flour	1 pkg. dates, chopped
1 tsp. soda	1 c. chopped nuts

Pour the butter into a mixing bowl. Add the sugar and eggs and beat well. Sift the flour with soda. Add remaining ingredients and mix until coated. Add to sugar mixture and mix well. Drop by small teaspoonfuls onto a greased cookie sheet. Bake at 350 degrees for 10 to 12 minutes.

Mrs. L. F. Cooper, Marlow, Oklahoma

TEA CAKES

3 c. sugar	3 eggs
1 c. shortening	1/4 tsp. salt
1 tsp. soda	1/2 tsp. nutmeg
1 c. buttermilk	4 c. flour

Cream the sugar and shortening in a bowl. Dissolve the soda in buttermilk, then stir into the creamed mixture. Beat in the eggs, one at a time. Stir in remaining ingredients. Roll out on a floured pastry cloth and cut with cookie cutter. Place on a greased cookie sheet. Bake at 350 degrees for 12 to 15 minutes or until golden brown.

Mrs. Guy H. Smith, McCoy, Texas

MINCEMEAT SQUARES

1 c. (packed) brown sugar	3/4 c. shortening
1 1/4 c. rolled oats	2 c. mincemeat
1 1/2 c. flour	1 egg yolk
1/2 tsp. salt	

Combine the brown sugar, oats, flour and salt in a bowl and mix well. Cut in shortening with 2 knives or a pastry blender until mixture is consistency of coarse crumbs. Spread 1/2 of the mixture in 9 x 9 x 2-inch pan. Cover with mincemeat and spread remaining oats mixture on mincemeat. Beat the egg yolk with 1 tablespoon water and brush on oats mixture. Bake at 400 degrees for 20 to 25 minutes. Cool and cut into squares.

Mrs. Mary P. Murray, DeFuniak Springs, Florida

CREPES SUZETTE

1 c. flour	Butter
1 c. milk	Sugar
1/2 c. water	1 tbsp. confectioners' sugar
1 egg	Juice of 1 orange
1/2 tsp. salt	3/4 c. orange liqueur
1/2 tbsp. salad oil	1 tbsp. grated orange peel
Cognac	1 tsp. grated lemon peel

Place the flour in a bowl. Add the milk and water and beat until smooth. Add the egg, salt, oil and 1/2 tablespoon cognac and beat until smooth. Refrigerate overnight. Melt just enough butter in a small frying pan to cover bottom. Add the batter, using 1 tablespoon for each crepe, and cook until golden brown on both sides, turning once. Sprinkle lightly with sugar. Melt 1/4 cup butter in a chafing dish over hot flame. Add the confectioners' sugar and orange juice and cook until sugar is dissolved. Add the orange liqueur, orange peel and lemon peel and bring to a boil. Place the crepes, one at a time, in the chafing dish and fold each crepe twice. Add 3/4 cup cognac and bring to a boil. Ignite. Ladle over crepes until the flame is extinguished. Serve the crepes on warm plates and spoon the sauce over crepes.

Mrs. Anne Jennings, New Orleans, Louisiana

CREME DE FRAISE

1 1/2 c. sugar	2 c. milk
3 tbsp. flour	1 tsp. vanilla
Pinch of salt	3 tbsp. melted butter
4 eggs, separated	Sliced drained strawberries

Sift 1 cup sugar, flour and salt together into a mixing bowl. Add egg yolks and mix well. Stir in the milk slowly. Stir in vanilla and butter and pour into a greased 9-inch square baking pan. Bake at 325 degrees for 45 minutes or until set and brown. Cover top with strawberries. Beat the egg whites in a bowl until stiff, adding remaining sugar gradually, then spread over strawberries. Return to oven and bake until meringue is brown.

Mrs. Howard Greer, Jackson, Georgia

CREOLE PRALINES

1 c. (packed) brown sugar	2 tbsp. butter or margarine
1 c. sugar	1 c. broken pecans
1/2 c. cream	

Combine the sugars and cream in a saucepan and cook to soft-ball stage or 238 degrees on candy thermometer, stirring occasionally. Add the butter and pecans and remove from heat. Beat until mixture starts to thicken. Drop from teaspoon onto a greased surface.

Mrs. A. V. Rachal, Alexandria, Louisiana

BOURBON BALLS

1 6-oz. package semisweet chocolate morsels	1/3 c. bourbon 2 1/2 c. finely crushed
1/2 c. sugar	vanilla wafers
3 tbsp. light corn syrup	1 c. finely chopped walnuts

Melt the chocolate morsels in top of a double boiler over hot, not boiling, water, then remove from water. Stir in the sugar and corn syrup and blend in the bourbon. Combine the wafer crumbs and walnuts in a bowl. Add the chocolate mixture and mix well. Shape into 1-inch balls and roll in additional sugar. Let ripen in covered container for several days. 4 1/2 dozen.

BUTTERSCOTCH PRALINES

2 c. sugar	1 6-oz. package
1 c. (firmly packed) light brown sugar	butterscotch morsels 1/4 c. coarsely chopped
1/4 c. light corn syrup	walnuts
1 tsp. vinegar	1/4 c. hot water
1/2 tsp. salt	

Combine the sugars, 3/4 cup water, corn syrup, vinegar and salt in 2-quart saucepan and bring to a full boil, stirring constantly. Cook over high heat for 3 minutes without stirring. Remove from heat. Add the butterscotch morsels and beat until morsels are melted. Mixture will be thin. Stir in the walnuts. Drop by tablespoonfuls on ungreased foil or heavy brown paper, stirring in small amount of water if mixture becomes too thick. Let stand at room temperature or chill until set. 4 dozen.

Bourbon Balls (above)
Butterscotch Pralines (above)

OLD-FASHIONED SOUTHERN CUSTARD

3 qt. milk	1 tbsp. (heaping) flour
1 c. cream	Pinch of salt
10 eggs, separated	1 tbsp. vanilla
2 c. sugar	

Mix the milk and cream in a large double boiler and heat until scalded. Beat the egg yolks well. Mix the sugar, flour and salt and add to the egg yolks. Mix well. Add small amount of milk mixture, beating constantly. Stir back into milk mixture and cook for 10 minutes, stirring constantly. Fold in stiffly beaten egg whites. Add vanilla and cool. Chill.

Clara Lee Webb, Amber, Oklahoma

HOMEMADE PEACH ICE CREAM

6 c. chopped peaches	3 eggs, beaten
2 1/2 c. sugar	1 qt. milk
2 tbsp. flour	1/2 pt. whipping cream
1/2 tsp. salt	1 tbsp. vanilla

Sweeten peaches with 1 cup sugar. Combine remaining sugar, flour and salt in a saucepan and blend in eggs. Add the milk and cook over low heat until slightly thickened, stirring constantly. Cool. Add the cream, vanilla and peaches and pour into freezer. Freeze. 1 gallon.

Mrs. Drew Robbins, Rocky Mount, North Carolina

LEMON ICE

2 1/2 c. water	1 tbsp. grated lemon rind
3/4 c. light corn syrup	2/3 c. lemon juice
1 c. sugar	Yellow food coloring
1/4 tsp. salt	

Combine the water, corn syrup, sugar, salt and lemon rind in a saucepan and cook over low heat, stirring, until sugar is dissolved. Bring to a boil and cook for 5 minutes without stirring. Cool. Add lemon juice and strain into a refrigerator tray. Tint a delicate yellow with food coloring, then freeze until partially frozen. Remove to a chilled bowl and break into lumps. Beat with rotary beater or electric mixer until light. Return to refrigerator tray and freeze until firm.

Dixie Lindsay, Jackson, Tennessee

MARVELOUS VANILLA ICE CREAM

5 lge. eggs	2 tsp. vanilla
2 1/3 c. sugar	1/2 gal. milk
1 lge. can evaporated milk	

Beat the eggs in a bowl with electric mixer at high speed until thick. Add sugar and beat until well mixed. Add remaining ingredients and mix well. Freeze in 1-gallon mechanical freezer according to freezer directions.

Mrs. B. B. Sherrill, Riceville, Tennessee

PISTACHIO ICE CREAM

24 marshmallows	1 c. heavy cream, whipped
1 c. milk	1 c. chopped pistachio nuts
3 drops of oil of peppermint	1 can sliced peaches, drained
1/8 tsp. salt	Purple grape clusters
Green food coloring	

Place the marshmallows and milk in top of a double boiler and cook over hot water until marshmallows are melted, stirring frequently. Remove from water and cool slightly. Stir in the oil of peppermint, salt and enough food coloring to tint light green and chill until thickened. Fold in the whipped cream and pistachio nuts and spoon into a 1-quart ice cream container or mold. Freeze until firm. Unmold onto a serving dish and garnish with peaches and grapes.

Photograph for this recipe on page 140.

AMBROSIA

1 fresh coconut	1 c. sugar
1 doz. oranges	Powdered sugar

Remove the milk from coconut. Remove the shell and cut off brown portion. Grate the coconut. Peel and slice the oranges. Remove the seeds. Place a layer of oranges in a large glass dish and sprinkle with some of the sugar. Add a layer of coconut. Repeat layers until all of the oranges, sugar and coconut are used, ending with coconut. Sprinkle with powdered sugar and chill for about 2 hours.

Mrs. Nita Morgan, Shreveport, Louisiana

STRAWBERRIES CHANTILLY

1 qt. fresh strawberries	2 egg whites
Confectioners' sugar	Sweetened whipped cream
2 tbsp. rum	

Wash the strawberries. Stem and cut in half. Place in a bowl and cover with confectioners' sugar. Add the rum and chill for 30 minutes. Beat the egg whites in a bowl until stiff peaks form, adding 4 tablespoons confectioners' sugar gradually. Fold in the strawberries. Place in 6 sherbet glasses and top with whipped cream.

Mrs. Adrian Blake, Atlanta, Georgia

FRESH APPLE TRIFLE

8 c. sliced tart apples	1 lge. egg, beaten
2 tbsp. water	1 c. milk
Sugar	1/2 tsp. vanilla
Salt	12 ladyfingers
1/2 tsp. ground nutmeg	1/2 c. heavy cream, whipped
1 tsp. grated lemon peel	

Place the apples and water in a saucepan and cover. Cook over low heat until apples are tender. Remove from heat and press through a sieve. Add 3/4 cup sugar, 1/4 teaspoon salt, nutmeg and lemon peel and mix well. Cool. Combine 2 tablespoons sugar and a dash of salt in top of a double boiler. Add the egg and mix until blended. Stir in the milk and cook over hot water, stirring constantly, until custard coats a spoon. Remove from heat and stir in vanilla. Cool, then chill. Place alternate layers of ladyfingers, apple mixture and custard in a casserole. Refrigerate until chilled. Mix whipped cream with 1 tablespoon sugar and spread on chilled mixure.

Mrs. W. M. Smith, Prattville, Alabama

DEEP-DISH CHERRY-ALMOND SHORTCAKES

1 1-lb. 1-oz. can pitted dark sweet cherries	1/4 tsp. salt
Sugar	3 tbsp. butter or margarine
2 tbsp. cornstarch	1/4 c. finely chopped almonds
1/4 tsp. almond extract	1 c. biscuit mix
2 tsp. lemon juice	1/3 c. milk

Deep-Dish Cherry-Almond Shortcakes (above)

Drain the cherries and reserve syrup. Add enough water to reserved syrup to make 1 cup liquid and pour into a saucepan. Mix 1/4 cup sugar and cornstarch and stir into cherry syrup mixture. Bring to a boil. Reduce heat and cook, stirring, until thickened and smooth. Add the almond extract, lemon juice, salt and 1 tablespoon butter and turn into 4 individual serving dishes. Cool. Mix the almonds, 1 teaspoon sugar and biscuit mix in a mixing bowl and cut in remaining butter. Add the milk and mix well. Roll out on a floured board to 3/8-inch thickness and cut into 4 rounds or other shapes. Place on a cookie sheet. Bake in 425-degree oven for 8 to 10 minutes or until golden brown. Sprinkle with sugar. Place on cherry filling. Pitted sour red cherries may be substituted for sweet cherries. Increase sugar to 1/2 cup and add several drops of red food coloring to sauce. Garnish with whole almonds and pitted cherries, if desired.

BLACKBERRY PIE

Pastry for 2-crust pie	1/4 tsp. salt
2 c. blackberries	1/4 c. water
Flour	4 tbsp. butter
1 c. sugar	

Line a 10-inch pie plate with pastry. Place the blackberries in the pastry and sprinkle lightly with flour. Sprinkle with sugar and salt. Add the water and dot with butter. Cover with top crust and seal edge. Cut slits in the center of the crust. Bake at 375 degrees until brown.

Mrs. Charles E. Barnes, Marion, Alabama

MOLASSES PIE

1 1/2 c. molasses	3 eggs
1/2 c. buttermilk	1 unbaked pie crust
1/2 c. butter	

Mix all ingredients except pie crust in a bowl, then pour into the pie crust. Bake at 325 degrees until a knife inserted in the center comes out clean.

Mrs. Effie Howard, Bellaire, Texas

PLUM PUDDING

1 c. boiling water	3/4 c. sugar
1/2 c. mincemeat	1 c. chopped nuts
1 tsp. soda	2 egg yolks
1 c. bread crumbs	

Mix the boiling water and mincemeat in a bowl. Add remaining ingredients and mix well. Place in a greased square pan. Bake at 350 degrees for about 35 minutes. Cut into squares and top with whipped cream or dessert topping and a cherry, if desired.

Mrs. Bruce Nance, Dalhart, Texas

Caramel-Topped Rice Pudding (below)

CARAMEL-TOPPED RICE PUDDING

3 eggs, beaten slightly
1/2 c. sugar
3/4 tsp. salt
1/2 tsp. nutmeg
3 c. milk
1/4 c. butter

1 c. cooked rice
1 tsp. vanilla
1/2 tsp. rum extract
1/3 c. slivered almonds
1/2 c. (firmly packed)
   brown sugar

Mix the eggs, sugar, salt and nutmeg well. Combine the milk and 2 tablespoons butter in a saucepan and heat until scalded. Pour into egg mixture slowly, stirring constantly. Stir in the rice, vanilla and rum extract and pour into a shallow 1 1/2-quart casserole. Place in a shallow pan of hot water. Bake at 350 degrees for 30 minutes or until knife inserted in center comes out clean. Remove pudding from oven and hot water. Brown almonds lightly in remaining butter and stir in the brown sugar. Sprinkle over the pudding. Broil about 3 inches from heat until hot and bubbly, then cool slightly. Serve warm or cold. 6-8 servings.

SWEET POTATO PUDDING

1 c. sugar
1 c. (packed) brown sugar
2 c. milk
3 c. grated sweet potatoes
4 eggs, beaten

1/4 stick margarine, melted
1/2 c. raisins
1 1/2 c. chopped pecans
1 c. shredded coconut

Combine all ingredients in a bowl and mix well. Pour into 8 x 8 x 2-inch baking pan. Bake at 350 degrees for 1 hour. 10-12 servings.

Mrs. Fred W. Ross, Indian Trail, North Carolina

RICE PUDDING SUPREME

2 c. milk	**1/4 tsp. salt**
2 1/4 c. cooked rice	**1/2 c. raisins**
1 tbsp. butter	**3 eggs, beaten**
1/3 c. sugar	

Scald the milk in a saucepan and add the rice and butter. Mix the sugar, salt and raisins with eggs and stir into rice mixture slowly. Pour into a greased baking dish and set in pan of hot water. Bake at 350 degrees for 1 hour.

Hot Chocolate Sauce

1 sq. chocolate	**1/2 c. sugar**
1 tbsp. butter	**1/8 tsp. salt**
1/4 c. cream	**1/2 tsp. vanilla**

Melt the chocolate in a pan over hot water. Add the butter, cream, sugar and salt and stir until sugar is dissolved. Cook for 5 minutes, stirring constantly, then add vanilla. Serve over pudding. 4 servings.

Mrs. R. P. Smith, Victoria, Virginia

CAFE AU LAIT

4 c. milk	**Sugar to taste**
2 c. strong hot coffee	

Pour the milk into a saucepan and bring to boiling point. Remove from heat. Pour the milk and coffee into cups simultaneously, then sweeten with sugar.

Mrs. Grace Worthington, Sarasota, Florida

CAFE BRULOT

1 1/2 c. brandy	**8 whole allspice**
2 strips lemon peel	**2　2-in. sticks cinnamon**
1 strip orange peel	**8 cubes sugar**
8 whole cloves	**3 c. hot strong coffee**

Mix the brandy, lemon peel, orange peel, cloves, allspice and cinnamon in a blazer pan and heat through. Heat a ladle with boiling water and drain. Remove peels and spices from the brandy mixture. Add 7 cubes sugar to the brandy mixture and place remaining cube in the ladle. Place a small amount of the brandy mixture in the ladle and ignite. Lower the ladle into the chafing dish carefully and ignite all of the brandy mixture. Stir with the ladle carefully, dipping and pouring back into the pan, until the sugar is dissolved. Pour the hot coffee slowly against edge of the chafing dish to avoid extinguishing the flames. Ladle into demitasse cups when mixture is no longer flaming. Serve with additional sugar, if desired. 16 servings.

Mrs. Charlotte Dyess, North Little Rock, Arkansas

FRENCH HOT CHOCOLATE

6 oz. unsweetened chocolate	**3 qt. milk, scalded**
1 c. sugar	**4 c. sweetened whipped cream**

Place the chocolate in top of a double boiler and heat over boiling water until melted. Stir in the sugar and small amount of milk until smooth. Stir in remaining milk and beat with an electric mixer until frothy. Serve topped with whipped cream.

Mrs. Lillian Kite, Elkton, Virginia

CREOLE COFFEE

8 to 16 tbsp. drip grind	**4 c. water**
chicory coffee	

Fill a drip coffee maker with boiling water, then drain. Place the coffee in filter section of the coffee maker. Pour the water into a saucepan and bring to a boil. Pour 2 tablespoons water over the coffee and let all of the water drip through. Repeat the small additions of boiling water 5 times. Place the coffee maker over very low heat and repeat additions of water until all water is used. Do not let coffee boil. Remove the filter section and stir the coffee. Cover and serve. Place coffee maker over very low heat if coffee is not served immediately.

Mrs. Meg Smith, Silver City, New Mexico

SOUTHERN PLANTER'S PUNCH

2 tbsp. dark Jamaican rum	**Juice of 1 lemon**
1 tsp. brown sugar	**1 c. sweet red wine**

Pour the rum over shaved ice in a tall glass. Mix the brown sugar with 1 tablespoon water and add to the glass. Add lemon juice and wine and mix. Garnish with mint sprigs and fresh fruit.

Mrs. Linda Rivers, Greenville, South Carolina

MINT JULIP

1 c. mint leaves	**Rum**
8 tsp. sugar	**Confectioners' sugar**

Place tall silver goblets on a tray and place in refrigerator until chilled. Crush the mint leaves in a bowl with the sugar. Place shaved ice in the goblets, then place 2 layers of mint in each goblet. Fill the goblets with rum and stir with a long spoon until frosted. Sprinkle confectioners' sugar on top and garnish with fresh sprigs of mint.

Mrs. Hazel Meredith, Hickory, North Carolina

Two-Tone Coffee Cream (below)

TWO-TONE COFFEE CREAM

1 env. unflavored gelatin	2 tbsp. instant coffee
1/2 c. sugar	1 tsp. vanilla
1/8 tsp. salt	1/2 c. whipping cream,
2 c. scalded milk	whipped (opt.)
2 eggs, separated	

Mix the gelatin, 1/4 cup sugar and salt in top of a double boiler. Add hot milk to beaten egg yolks gradually, stirring constantly. Stir in the coffee, then stir into gelatin mixture. Cook over boiling water, stirring constantly, for about 10 minutes or until gelatin is dissolved and mixture is slightly thickened. Remove from water and add vanilla. Cool slightly. Beat the egg whites in a bowl until stiff, adding remaining sugar gradually. Fold into the gelatin mixture and pour into parfait or sherbet glasses. Let stand until mixture separates into 2 layers. Place in refrigerator until chilled. Serve topped with whipped cream. 6 servings.

MILK AU DIABLE

5 drops of hot sauce	1 c. cold milk

Stir the hot sauce into the milk and serve.

Mrs. Lamar Moody, Lawton, Oklahoma

Top: East Indian Dip (page 158)
Bottom: South Sea Delight (page 158)

creole sauces

Serving a meal in the Creole household was considered to be an art. An important part of that art was the complementary sauces and accompaniments. Each was carefully chosen to highlight this or that feature of the meal — the texture of a particularly fine piece of game or fowl, the freshness of a just-picked vegetable, or the richness of a dessert.

The recipes used to prepare sauces and accompaniments were as carefully and as painstakingly developed as any of the Creole repertoire — and some of the best of these are featured in this section. There is a recipe for Brown Roux, a blend of flour and butter that was indispensable to the creation of sauces. In fact, the roux, along with the iron pot, seasonings, and spirits, has been considered one of the four essential elements of Creole cookery! There are recipes for Bearnaise Sauce, delicious with steaks or any beef dish . . . Mushroom Sauce, a staple at Creole tables . . . hotly-seasoned Creole Sauce . . . and more.

Accompaniments are featured, too, with recipes for Hot-Tangy Mushrooms, an unusual way to prepare a favorite Creole food. Feature Quick Pickled Peaches and Pickled Okra at your table, and bring the spirit of Creole cookery to every member of your family. Depend on the recipes you'll find in this section and you'll be able to serve authentic Creole sauces and accompaniments at every meal.

Mustard-Cream Dip (below)

MUSTARD-CREAM DIP

1/2 c. sour cream	2 tsp. dillweed
1/4 c. prepared mustard	1/4 tsp. salt

Combine all ingredients and place in a serving bowl. Serve with hot French fries.

SOUTH SEA DELIGHT

2 c. sour cream	1/2 tsp. salt
4 green onions with tops, minced	1 c. flaked coconut
2 tsp. curry powder	1 6 to 8-oz. can crab meat, flaked
Dash of pepper	

Combine all ingredients in a bowl and chill for several hours to blend flavors. Serve with assorted crackers and chips. 3 cups.

Photograph for this recipe on page 156.

EAST INDIAN DIP

1 tsp. lemon juice	1/8 tsp. ginger
1/8 tsp. dry mustard	1/4 tsp. salt
1/2 tsp. curry powder	1 c. sour cream
Dash of garlic salt	

Combine the lemon juice and seasonings in a bowl and fold in the sour cream. Refrigerate for 1 hour or longer to blend flavors. Serve with fresh fruit. 1 cup.

Photograph for this recipe on page 156.

BARBECUE SAUCE

2 sm. onions, chopped	1 1/2 tsp. chili powder
1/4 c. margarine	2 tbsp. prepared mustard
2 tbsp. vinegar	1 c. catsup
1/2 c. steak sauce	1 tsp. sugar
2 tbsp. Worcestershire sauce	Salt and pepper to taste

Cook the onions in margarine in a saucepan until tender. Add remaining ingredients and bring to a boil. Remove from heat. May be refrigerated for 2 weeks.

Mrs. F. E. Cannon, Little Mountain, South Carolina

BASTING SAUCE FOR ROASTS

1/2 c. red wine	1/4 tsp. rosemary
1/2 c. hot water	1/2 tsp. marjoram or basil
1 tbsp. butter	1/2 tsp. salt
1 tbsp. olive oil	1/4 tsp. pepper
1/2 tsp. thyme	

Mix all ingredients in a saucepan and simmer for 10 minutes. Baste beef, lamb, pork, or veal roasts with sauce frequently while baking.

Mrs. Lucius Eaton, Dover, Delaware

BROWN GRAVY

2 tbsp. butter	1 c. brown stock or water
1 sm. onion, chopped (opt.)	1/2 tsp. salt
2 1/2 tbsp. flour	1/4 tsp. pepper

Melt the butter in a saucepan. Add the onion and cook until onion is light brown. Blend in the flour and cook, stirring, until flour is brown. Add the stock gradually and stir in the salt and pepper. Boil for 3 minutes, stirring constantly.

Mrs. Hope Jefferson, Rockville, Maryland

BROWN ROUX

2 tbsp. lard	4 tbsp. flour

Melt the lard in a skillet. Add flour and cook over low heat, stirring constantly, until dark brown.

Mrs. Seth Agee, Williamsburg, Kentucky

BEARNAISE SAUCE

2 cloves of garlic, minced	1 c. minced chives
2 c. white wine	1/2 tsp. rosemary
2 tbsp. margarine	3 egg yolks, beaten
1 tbsp. flour	1 c. chopped parsley

Place the garlic in the wine and let stand for 1 hour. Melt the margarine in a saucepan. Add the flour and cook until dark brown, stirring constantly. Add chives and rosemary. Stir in the wine mixture, small amount at a time, and simmer for 10 minutes. Cool, then stir in the egg yolks and minced parsley. One cup tomato paste may be added, if desired.

Mrs. Daisy Trammel, Portsmouth, Virginia

CHERRY SAUCE

1 No. 2 can red tart cherries	1/4 tsp. cloves
1/2 c. sugar	1/4 tsp. red food coloring
2 tbsp. cornstarch	

Drain the cherries and reserve liquid. Mix the sugar, cornstarch and cloves in a saucepan and stir in reserved liquid gradually. Cook, stirring constantly, until thick. Add the food coloring and cherries. Serve with ham. 6 servings.

Mrs. Walter D. Eyrich, Verona, Pennsylvania

CLARIFIED BUTTER

Butter

Melt the butter in a saucepan over low heat. Remove from heat and let stand until solids have settled in bottom of the saucepan. Skim clear butter from top and place in a container.

Mrs. Andrew Guran, Montgomery, Alabama

CREOLE COCKTAIL SAUCE

1/2 c. chili sauce	1/4 tsp. salt
1/2 c. catsup	2 tsp. lemon juice
1/4 c. horseradish	1/2 c. minced celery
1 1/2 tsp. Worcestershire sauce	1/4 tsp. cayenne pepper

Mix all ingredients in a bowl and refrigerate until chilled.

Mrs. D. W. Griffith, Grand Chenier, Louisiana

CURRY SAUCE

1/2 c. mayonnaise	1 tbsp. curry powder
2 tbsp. milk	1/4 tsp. hot sauce

Combine all ingredients in a bowl and refrigerate until chilled. 1/2 cup.

Mrs. H. F. Pickens, Laurel, Mississippi

BASIC CREOLE SAUCE

1/4 c. chopped green pepper	1 tbsp. brown sugar
1/2 c. chopped green onions	1 bay leaf
2 stalks celery, chopped	Pinch of basil
1 clove of garlic, minced	Pinch of rosemary
3 tbsp. bacon drippings	Pinch of thyme
1 No. 2 can tomatoes	Pinch of marjoram
Salt to taste	1 tbsp. Worcestershire sauce
Cayenne pepper to taste	2 tbsp. lemon juice (opt.)
1 can tomato sauce	

Saute the green pepper, onions, celery and garlic in bacon drippings in a saucepan until brown. Add the tomatoes and remaining ingredients and simmer for 40 minutes, stirring frequently. 2 1/2 cups.

Mrs. W. D. Bennett, Nashville, Tennessee

CURRANT SAUCE

1/2 c. red currant jelly	1/2 tsp. Worcestershire sauce
1/4 c. port	2 tbsp. butter or margarine
1/4 c. catsup	

Combine all ingredients in a small saucepan and cook over low heat until jelly is melted, stirring frequently. 1 cup.

Mrs. Frederick Hare, Morgantown, West Virginia

DELUXE STEAK BUTTER

1/4 lb. butter	1 tsp. lemon juice
1/4 tsp. garlic powder	1/4 tsp. pepper
1 tsp. minced green onion	1 tsp. paprika
1 tsp. dillweed	

Soften the butter in a bowl, then blend in the garlic powder, green onion, dillweed, lemon juice, pepper and paprika.

Marianna Thompson, Fort Smith, Arkansas

HARD SAUCE

1/3 c. butter	1 tsp. vanilla
1 c. powdered sugar	

Cream the butter in a bowl and stir in the sugar and vanilla. Refrigerate until chilled.

Mrs. Oliver Fowler, Thibodaux, Louisiana

161

HOLLANDAISE SAUCE

2 egg yolks, beaten	1/4 tsp. salt
2 tbsp. lemon juice	Paprika to taste
1/2 c. cold butter or margarine	

Mix the egg yolks and lemon juice in a saucepan. Add 1/4 cup butter, salt and paprika and cook over low heat, stirring constantly, until the butter is melted. Add remaining butter and cook, stirring, until the butter is melted and sauce is thickened.

Mrs. Troy White, Warrenton, North Carolina

HORSERADISH SAUCE FOR POT ROAST

1 c. sour cream	1 tbsp. orange marmalade
3 tbsp. horseradish	Salt to taste

Combine the sour cream, horseradish, orange marmalade and salt in a mixing bowl and mix well. 1 1/4 cups.

Mrs. Rozanna Vachon, Chevy Chase, Maryland

LAMB SAUCE

2 c. tomato paste	1 tbsp. vinegar
1 med. onion, minced	2 tbsp. olive oil
1 tsp. salt	1 tsp. oregano
1 tsp. pepper	1 green pepper, minced (opt.)

Mix all ingredients thoroughly in a bowl and chill. Serve with hot or cold barbecued lamb slices. 2 1/2 cups.

Mrs. W. D. Smith, Selma, Alabama

LEMON BUTTER

1/4 c. clarified butter	1 tsp. lemon juice
1 tbsp. chopped parsley	Salt to taste

Cook the butter in a saucepan over low heat until light brown. Remove from heat and add the parsley, lemon juice and salt.

Mrs. A. M. Nix, Marietta, Georgia

MINT SAUCE

3 tbsp. hot water	1/3 c. finely chopped mint
1 1/2 tsp. confectioners'	leaves
sugar	1/2 c. vinegar

Mix the water and sugar in a bowl until sugar is dissolved. Cool. Add remaining ingredients and mix well. Serve on lamb. 1 cup.

Mildred Franklin, Gadsden, Alabama

MORNAY SAUCE

4 tbsp. butter	1 c. cream
1 tbsp. finely chopped onion	2 egg yolks, beaten
3 tbsp. flour	1/2 c. grated Swiss cheese
3/4 c. chicken broth	

Heat 3 tablespoons butter in a heavy saucepan. Add the onion and cook until tender. Blend in the flour and heat until bubbly. Add the broth and cream gradually and bring to a boil, stirring constantly. Cook for 1 minute. Blend several tablespoons of the hot mixture into egg yolks, then stir back into the hot mixture. Stir in the cheese and remaining butter. Serve with fish. 4-6 servings.

Mrs. John Furlong, Long Beach, California

MUSHROOM SAUCE

1 pt. mushrooms	1 tsp. soy sauce
3 tbsp. butter	3/4 c. light cream
1 tbsp. flour	Salt and pepper to taste

Slice the mushrooms through cap and stem. Melt the butter in a skillet. Add the mushrooms and mix. Sprinkle the flour over mushrooms and mix. Cook over medium heat for 8 to 10 minutes or until mushrooms are tender, stirring occasionally. Add the soy sauce and stir in cream slowly. Cook, stirring until mixture thickens. Season with salt and pepper. 4 servings.

Katie Cannon, Pensacola, Florida

ORANGE SAUCE

1/2 c. orange juice	1/4 c. sugar
2 tbsp. lemon juice	1 tsp. cornstarch
1 tbsp. vinegar	1 tsp. cold water
1/2 tsp. salt	1 can mandarin oranges,
Dash of white pepper	drained
Dash of paprika	2 tbsp. butter

Combine the juices, vinegar, salt, pepper, paprika and sugar in top of a double boiler. Place over boiling water and heat through. Blend the cornstarch with the water, then stir into the sugar mixture. Cook until thickened. Add the orange sections and butter and mix well. Serve with ham or turkey. 2 1/2 cups.

Mrs. William Cooke, Bainbridge, Georgia

Pickle-Tomato Sauce (below)

PICKLE-TOMATO SAUCE

3/4 c. catsup
2 tbsp. finely chopped
   onion
1/4 c. sweet pickle liquid
1/4 c. water
2 tsp. flour

1 c. sweet cucumber pickles,
   cut in thin strips
1/2 tsp. Worcestershire
   sauce
Sweet cucumber pickle slices

Combine the catsup, onion, pickle liquid and water. Stir into flour in a saucepan slowly. Cook over low heat, stirring constantly, until slightly thickened. Stir in pickle strips and Worcestershire sauce. Serve hot or cold and garnish with pickle slices. About 2 cups.

MUSTARD SAUCE

1 c. sugar
3 eggs
1 tbsp. dry mustard
1/2 c. vinegar

1/2 c. water
1 tbsp. butter
Salt to taste

Mix the sugar, eggs and mustard in a saucepan. Add the vinegar and water and cook over low heat, stirring constantly, until thickened. Remove from heat. Add the butter and salt and mix well. 8-10 servings.

Mrs. F. R. Houmiel, Norfolk, Virginia

RAISIN SAUCE

1/2 c. (packed) brown sugar
1 tsp. dry mustard
2 tbsp. cornstarch
1/2 tbsp. salt

1/4 tsp. cloves
Dash of mace
Dash of nutmeg
Dash of cinnamon

1/4 tsp. grated lemon rind	1/4 c. vinegar
1/2 c. raisins	1 1/2 c. water

Mix first 8 ingredients in a saucepan. Add the lemon rind, raisins, vinegar and water and cook to syrup stage. Serve hot.

Deanna Brosten, McFarland, California

SAUCE PIQUANT

2 tbsp. olive oil	1 6-oz. can tomato paste
1/4 c. flour	1 tsp. salt
1 c. chopped onion	1/2 tsp. pepper
1 c. chopped celery	Dash of hot sauce
1 c. chopped green pepper	4 tbsp. Worcestershire sauce
2 8-oz. cans tomato sauce	1/2 tsp. brown sugar
2 c. water	1 tbsp. instant chicken bouillon

Combine the oil and flour and cook, stirring, until lightly browned. Add the onion, celery and green pepper and cook until soft, stirring frequently. Stir in remaining ingredients and cook for about 20 minutes. Serve warm over baked or smoked fish.

Mrs. W. J. Morgan, Houston, Texas

SOUR CREAM SAUCE

1/2 c. sour cream	2 tbsp. sweet relish
2 tbsp. mayonnaise	

Combine all ingredients in a bowl and mix well. Serve with sweetbreads or cold meat slices.

Mrs. Edward M. Blakeman, Frankfort, Kentucky

SUPERB GAME SAUCE

1 stick margarine, melted	4 tbsp. brown sugar
1/2 bottle catsup	Dash of monosodium glutamate
1 tsp. pepper	3 tsp. paprika
1/2 c. vinegar	Juice of 2 lemons (opt.)
3 tbsp. Worcestershire sauce	1 tbsp. horseradish (opt.)
2 cloves of garlic, minced	1 tbsp. mustard
1/2 tsp. liquid smoke (opt.)	3 tbsp. cognac
1/2 tsp. hot sauce (opt.)	

Combine all ingredients in a saucepan and simmer for at least 30 minutes. May be refrigerated and reheated.

Mrs. W. D. King, Charleston, South Carolina

SWEET AND SOUR SAUCE

1/4 c. (packed) brown sugar	1 green pepper, cut in strips
1/4 c. vinegar	1/2 c. water
3 tbsp. cornstarch	1 tsp. salt
1 tbsp. soy sauce	1/2 lemon, sliced
2 tbsp. Worcestershire sauce	1 bay leaf
1 tsp. chili powder	1 tsp. marjoram
3/4 c. red wine	1 tsp. thyme
1 c. catsup	2 onions, chopped
1/2 can chunk pineapple, drained	1 clove of garlic

Mix all ingredients in a saucepan and simmer for 45 minutes. Remove garlic, bay leaf and lemon slices just before serving. 8 servings.

Mrs. A. L. Gunter, Lake Wales, Florida

TARTAR SAUCE

1 2/3 c. mayonnaise	1 1/2 tbsp. minced onion
3 tbsp. chopped pickle relish	1 tbsp. minced parsley
3 tbsp. chopped stuffed olives	2 tsp. vinegar

Place all ingredients in a bowl and mix well. Chill. Serve with seafood. 2 cups.

Mrs. Judy Mulkey Waite, Cantonment, Florida

TOMATO GRAVY

2 lge. green peppers	2 6-oz. cans tomato paste
6 stalks celery	1 tbsp. dried parsley flakes
2 green onions	1 tsp. dried mint flakes
1 med. white onion	2 tsp. cinnamon
6 tbsp. olive oil	1 tbsp. salt
3 tbsp. minced garlic	2 tsp. oregano
2 15-oz. cans tomatoes	2 tsp. aniseed

Chop the green peppers, celery, green onions and onion and place in a large skillet in the olive oil. Add the garlic and cook until light brown, stirring constantly. Add 8 cups boiling water and remaining ingredients and cook until thickened, stirring occasionally.

Mrs. Ned Byron, Austin, Texas

CHILI SAUCE

2 pods of hot pepper	3 green peppers, seeded
40 ripe tomatoes, peeled	5 c. sugar
6 apples, cored	2 c. vinegar
10 sm. onions, peeled	Salt to taste
3 red peppers, seeded	3 tbsp. allspice

Grind the first 6 ingredients in a food chopper and place in a kettle. Stir in the sugar, vinegar and salt. Tie the allspice in a cheesecloth bag and add to the tomato mixture. Bring to a boil and reduce heat. Simmer for 1 hour or until thickened, stirring occasionally. Remove the cheesecloth bag. Place the chili sauce in sterilized jars and seal.

Mrs. Sandra Shears, Elizabeth, West Virginia

MEDIUM WHITE SAUCE

2 tbsp. butter	1/2 tsp. salt
2 tbsp. flour	1 c. milk

Melt the butter in a saucepan and stir in the flour and salt. Stir in the milk gradually and cook, stirring, until mixture comes to a boil. Cook for 3 minutes, stirring frequently.

Frances Clinton, Tulsa, Oklahoma

APPLE-TOMATO JELLY

1 1/4 c. apple juice	3 dashes of hot sauce
1 c. tomato juice	1/4 tsp. ground cloves
5 c. sugar	1/2 bottle liquid fruit
1/2 c. lemon juice	pectin
1/2 tsp. onion juice	

Combine the apple juice, tomato juice, sugar, lemon juice, onion juice, hot sauce and cloves in a large saucepan. Place over high heat and bring to a boil, stirring constantly. Stir in liquid fruit pectin at once, then bring to a full rolling boil and boil for 1 minute, stirring constantly. Remove from heat and skim off foam with a metal spoon. Pour into sterilized jelly glasses quickly and cover at once with 1/8 inch hot paraffin. About 6 glasses.

Left: Apple-Tomato Jelly (above)
Right: Applesauce-Ginger Jam (page 168)

167

APPLESAUCE-GINGER JAM

4 c. canned applesauce	4 tbsp. lemon juice
4 1/2 c. sugar	1/8 tsp. cinnamon
1/2 c. chopped crystallized ginger	1/8 tsp. powdered ginger
	1 bottle liquid fruit pectin

Combine the applesauce, sugar, crystallized ginger, lemon juice, cinnamon and powdered ginger in a large saucepan. Place over high heat and bring to a boil, stirring constantly. Stir in liquid fruit pectin at once, then bring to a full, rolling boil and boil for 1 minute, stirring constantly. Remove from heat and skim off foam with a metal spoon. Pour into sterilized jelly glasses quickly and cover at once with 1/8 inch hot paraffin. About 11 glasses.

Photograph for this recipe on page 167.

BRANDIED PEARS

12 fresh Bartlett pears	1/2 tsp. nutmeg
1 c. (packed) light brown sugar	Brandy
1 1/8 c. sugar	2 sticks butter or margarine
1 tsp. cinnamon	1 egg yolk

Peel the pears, leaving stems intact. Mix brown sugar, 2 tablespoons sugar, cinnamon and nutmeg in a bowl. Roll pears in sugar mixture and place upright in a large casserole. Pour 1 tablespoon brandy over each pear. Bake in 350-degree oven for 40 minutes. Cream the butter well. Add remaining sugar gradually, beating well, then stir in the egg yolk. Add 1 wine glass brandy, small amount at a time. Serve with pears.

Mrs. Whitney Edmonson Smith, Webb, Mississippi

CANDIED DRIED APRICOTS

2 1-lb. packages dried apricot halves	2 c. water
Sugar	2 tbsp. light corn syrup
	1/2 c. walnut halves

Wash the apricots and drain. Spread in single layer until dry. Mix 1 cup sugar, water and corn syrup in a saucepan. Bring to a boil and cook for about 15 minutes or until thickened. Add layer of apricots, cut side down, and cook over low heat for 5 minutes. Remove from saucepan with tongs and shake off excess syrup. Place on waxed paper and cool. Repeat with remaining apricots. Roll apricots in sugar and press a walnut half into center of each apricot. Place in layers in a container with waxed paper between each layer. Cover.

Mrs. Nicole Ausabee, Montgomery, Alabama

CRANBERRY-ORANGE RELISH

2 oranges, unpeeled	2 c. sugar
4 c. fresh cranberries	

Quarter and seed the oranges. Grind the orange quarters and cranberries through a food chopper and place in a bowl. Stir in the sugar and chill for several hours. 1 quart.

Mrs. Barbara Mixon, Dallas, Texas

PICKLED PRUNES

12 lge. dried prunes	1/2 c. sugar
12 English walnut halves	1 2-in. stick cinnamon
2/3 c. vinegar	6 whole cloves

Cook the prunes according to package directions until partially done. Drain and reserve 1/3 cup liquid. Cool the prunes. Cut a slit in the side of each prune and remove pits. Insert a walnut half and press cut edges together. Combine the vinegar, reserved liquid and sugar and cook for 5 minutes. Add the cinnamon, cloves and prunes and simmer until prunes are tender. Cool. Drain the prunes and refrigerate.

Mrs. William Mims, Richmond, Virginia

CURRIED FRUITS

1 No. 2 1/2 can peach halves	5 maraschino cherries, sliced
1 No. 2 1/2 can apricot halves	1/3 c. melted butter or margarine
1 can pineapple chunks	3/4 c. (packed) brown sugar
	Curry powder to taste

Drain all the fruits and arrange in casserole. Mix the butter, brown sugar and curry powder and spread on fruits. Bake in 325-degree oven for 1 hour. 6-8 servings.

Mrs. Conrad Sanders, Norfolk, Virginia

CHILLED BRANDIED FRUIT

2 lge. grapefruit	2 tbsp. sugar
4 lge. oranges	3 tbsp. brandy
2 c. halved grapes, seeded	

Peel the grapefruit and oranges and remove sections over a bowl. Drain the sections and reserve juice. Mound the grapes in center of a serving bowl and surround with grapefruit and orange sections. Mix the sugar and brandy and stir in reserved juice until sugar is dissolved. Pour over grape mixture and chill for several hours. 8-10 servings.

Mrs. Luther Pratt, Macon, Georgia

QUICK PICKLE PEACHES

1 No. 2 1/2 can peach halves	2 3-in. sticks cinnamon
3/4 c. (packed) brown sugar	1 tsp. whole cloves
1/2 c. vinegar	1 tsp. whole allspice

Drain the peaches and reserve syrup. Mix the reserved syrup, brown sugar, vinegar and spices in a saucepan and bring to a boil. Cook for 5 minutes. Add the peaches and simmer for 5 minutes longer. Place in refrigerator and let stand overnight. Drain the peaches before serving. 7-8 servings.

Mrs. Myrtle Daniel, Lobelville, Tennessee

SPICED ORANGE WEDGES

4 oranges, unpeeled	12 whole cloves
2 c. sugar	3 2-in. sticks cinnamon
1/2 c. vinegar	

Place the oranges in a saucepan and add 1 quart water. Bring to a boil and reduce heat. Simmer for 20 minutes. Drain and cut into eighths. Combine the sugar, 1 1/4 cups water, vinegar, cloves and cinnamon in the saucepan and cook over low heat, stirring, until sugar is dissolved. Bring to a boil and add the oranges. Simmer for about 20 minutes or until syrup is thick. Cool. Cover and chill.

Mrs. B. F. Parr, Spartanburg, South Carolina

ORANGE PECANS

2 c. sugar	Pinch of salt
3/4 c. orange juice	6 c. pecan halves
Grated rind of 2 oranges	

Combine the sugar, orange juice and grated rind in a saucepan and cook to soft-ball stage. Add salt and pecan halves and stir until pecans are coated. Place on waxed paper and separate pecans. Cool.

Edith Jenkins, Lake Village, Arkansas

OLD-FASHIONED CORN RELISH

1/4 c. sugar	1 12-oz. can whole kernel
1/2 c. vinegar	corn
1/2 tsp. salt	2 tbsp. chopped green pepper
1/4 tsp. hot sauce	1 tbsp. chopped pimento
1/2 tsp. celery seed	1 tbsp. minced onion
1/4 tsp. mustard seed	

Combine the sugar, vinegar, salt, hot sauce, celery seed and mustard seed in a saucepan. Bring to a boil and cook for 2 minutes. Remove from heat. Drain the corn and add to the vinegar mixture. Add remaining ingredients and mix. Place in a bowl and cover. Chill.

Mrs. Evelyn W. Newsom, Mt. Vernon, Texas

MARINATED EGGPLANT

1 sm. eggplant	1/8 tsp. powdered dill
1/2 c. chopped celery	1/4 tsp. oregano
1/3 c. chopped pimento	1/2 tsp. salt
1 sm. clove of garlic, minced	1/8 tsp. pepper
2 tbsp. chopped capers	1/3 c. salad oil
2 tbsp. chopped parsley	1/3 c. vinegar

Cook the eggplant in boiling, salted water for 20 minutes or until tender. Drain and cool. Peel the eggplant and cut into 2-inch lengths. Place in a bowl. Add remaining ingredients and mix well. Cover tightly and store in refrigerator. 6 servings.

Janell Bullard, Glenmora, Louisiana

ANTIPASTO WITH ITALIAN SEASONING

3/4 tsp. Italian seasoning	1 c. cottage cheese
1 c. French dressing	Thinly sliced cold cuts
Artichoke hearts, cooked	Melon wedges
Whole mushrooms, cooked	Carrot sticks

Mix 1/2 teaspoon Italian seasoning with the French dressing in a bowl. Add the artichoke hearts and mushrooms and toss lightly. Chill for several hours, tossing occasionally. Drain the artichoke hearts and mushrooms and reserve dressing. Mix the cottage cheese with remaining Italian seasoning and place in the center of a platter. Surround with the cold cuts, melon wedges, carrot sticks, artichoke hearts and mushrooms. Serve with reserved dressing.

Antipasto with Italian Seasoning (above)

PICKLED EGGS

3 doz. hard-cooked eggs	1 tsp. powdered ginger
2 pt. white vinegar	2 cloves of garlic
10 whole allspice	2 bay leaves
1 tbsp. salt	1 pod of red pepper

Remove the shells from eggs and place the eggs in a large jar. Place the vinegar and remaining ingredients in a saucepan and simmer for about 15 minutes. Pour over the eggs and cover. Let stand for at least 24 hours, then chill. Will keep indefinitely in refrigerator.

Mrs. Blanche Young, Pine Bluff, Arkansas

HOT TANGY MUSHROOMS

3 lb. fresh mushrooms	1 tbsp. oregano
3 cloves of garlic, diced	1 tsp. crushed hot red pepper
1/4 c. olive oil	1 c. wine

Place the mushrooms in a saucepan and cover with water. Bring to a boil and cook for 5 minutes. Drain. Brown the garlic in oil in the saucepan. Add the oregano, mushrooms, hot pepper and wine and simmer until mushrooms are tender, adding water, if needed.

Mrs. Jewel Harvey, Newport News, Virginia

MARINATED ONIONS

1 1/4 c. vinegar	2 tsp. salt
1/2 c. cooking oil	10 Spanish onions, thinly
1/2 c. sugar	sliced

Combine first 4 ingredients in a saucepan and heat, stirring until sugar and salt are dissolved. Place the onions in a large jar and pour in vinegar mixture. Refrigerate for several days, shaking jar occasionally.

Millie Brock, Baltimore, Maryland

PICKLED OKRA

2 lb. small okra	3 c. vinegar
4 tbsp. dillseed	1 1/2 c. water
4 cloves of garlic	1/2 c. salt

Trim tough stems from okra pods without cutting into seed pods. Pack in 4 sterilized pint jars. Add 1 tablespoon dillseed and 1 clove of garlic to each jar. Mix the vinegar, water and salt in saucepan and bring to boiling point. Pour over the okra and seal the jars. Let stand for 3 weeks. Chill before serving.

Mrs. Helen P. Sims, Spearsville, Louisiana

PICKLED SHRIMP

1 lb. cooked shrimp	1/3 c. catsup
2 med. onions, cut in rings	1/3 c. vinegar
3 or 4 bay leaves, crumbled	1 tsp. salt
1 c. salad oil	Dash of red pepper
2 tsp. sugar	Dash of hot sauce
1/2 tsp. dry mustard	1 clove of garlic, chopped
2 tbsp. Worcestershire sauce	

Place alternate layers of shrimp and onions in a bowl and add the bay leaves. Mix remaining ingredients and pour over shrimp mixture. Refrigerate for 24 hours.

Mrs. John Sawyer Barr, III, Oak Ridge, Louisiana

SPICED TOMATO MARMALADE

3 lb. ripe tomatoes	1/2 tsp. salt
3 lb. sugar	3 1-in. pieces gingerroot
2 fresh lemons	1/2 tsp. ground allspice
1 fresh orange	

Scald the tomatoes. Dip in cold water and remove skins. Cut into quarters and place in a 3-quart saucepan. There should be 7 1/2 cups. Add the sugar and let stand. Peel the lemons and orange. Cut fruit into small pieces and add to tomatoes. Cut rinds into thin, fine slivers and place in a saucepan. Cover with boiling water and boil for 10 minutes. Drain and add to tomatoes. Add the salt and ginger and bring to boiling point. Cook over medium-low heat for 35 minutes or until medium-thick and the rinds are transparent, stirring occasionally. Add the allspice and cook for 5 minutes longer. Ladle into hot, sterilized jars and seal at once. One-half teaspoon ground ginger may be added with allspice if gingerroot is not available. 2 1/2 pints.

Spiced Tomato Marmalade (above)

Coconut Praline Coffee Cake (Page 179)

creole breads

If Creole cookery shares one overriding characteristic in common with the rest of southern cooking, it is a love of breads. Many of the breads featured in Creole homes were distinctively French in origin; others were obvious borrowings from their southern neighbors. But all were prepared with an attention to detail and love of good food that is the hallmark of Creole cookery.

As you turn the pages of this section, you'll discover recipes that echo France — like the one for a crisp-crusted French Bread. Rice Griddle Cakes are an innovative version of pancakes prepared with a grain readily available in and around Louisiana.

Many other recipes are typical of those that could be found in southern homes from Maryland to Texas. Louisiana Hush Puppies are a local version of the cornmeal-based, fried bread served with fish and other dishes throughout the Southland. Beaten Biscuits and Old-Fashioned Southern Spoon Bread are two more recipes that show how Creole cookery, distinctive as it was, was still part of the South.

Explore these recipes, and envision how you can use them, as the great Creole cooks did — to highlight every dish and to complete every meal. Make yourself into an expert bread cook — and prepare yourself for warm compliments on the meals you serve, highlighted by Creole breads.

175

Currant Scones (below)

CURRANT SCONES

2 1/4 to 2 3/4 c. unsifted flour	1/2 c. milk
1 tbsp. sugar	1/2 c. water
1/2 tsp. salt	2 tbsp. margarine
1 pkg. dry yeast	1/2 c. currants

Mix 1 cup flour, sugar, salt and undissolved yeast thoroughly in a large bowl. Combine the milk, water and margarine in a saucepan and heat over low heat until liquids are warm. Margarine does not need to melt. Add to dry ingredients gradually and beat for 2 minutes with electric mixer at medium speed, scraping bowl occasionally. Add 1/2 cup flour and beat at high speed for 2 minutes, scraping bowl occasionally. Stir in the currants and enough remaining flour to make a soft dough. Turn out onto a lightly floured board and knead for 8 to 10 minutes or until smooth and elastic. Place in a greased bowl, turning to grease top, and cover. Let rise in a warm place, free from draft, for about 1 hour or until doubled in bulk. Punch down. Roll out on a lightly floured board to 1/2-inch thickness and cut with a 3-inch round cookie cutter. Cover and let rest for 30 minutes. Place on a lightly greased, medium hot griddle or on an electric griddle at 375 degrees and bake for about 20 minutes on each side or until well browned. Remove from griddle and place on wire racks to cool. Serve, split and toasted, with additional margarine and jam or jelly, if desired. 10 scones.

BEATEN BISCUITS

2 c. self-rising flour	1/4 c. shortening
1 tbsp. sugar	2/3 c. water

Blend the flour and sugar in a mixing bowl, then cut in the shortening until mixture resembles meal. Add the water, small amount at a time, and mix well. Turn out onto a lightly floured surface. Knead, then beat with a small mallet for

4 minutes. Roll out to 1-inch thickness and cut into 2-inch circles. Place on an ungreased cookie sheet. Bake at 400 degrees until lightly browned. 1 dozen.

Mrs. Lester Harris, Muskogee, Oklahoma

HOT BISCUITS

1 c. flour	2 tbsp. shortening
1 1/2 tsp. baking powder	1/2 c. milk
1/2 tsp. salt	Salad oil

Sift the dry ingredients together into a bowl and cut in shortening with a pastry blender. Add the milk and mix well. Roll out 3/4 inch thick on a floured surface and cut with a biscuit cutter. Place on a well-oiled baking sheet, turning once to coat top. Bake at 475 degrees for about 10 minutes.

Mrs. Hugh W. Sheffield, Dallas, Texas

SAUSAGE BISCUITS

1/2 lb. bulk sausage	1/4 c. shortening
2 c. self-rising flour	3/4 c. buttermilk

Crumble the sausage and cook in a skillet, stirring, until brown. Drain. Place the flour in a mixing bowl and cut in shortening. Add the buttermilk and stir until blended. Stir in the sausage. Knead on a floured board 10 times. Roll out to 1/2 inch thickness and cut with a biscuit cutter. Place on an ungreased cookie sheet. Bake at 450 degrees for 10 minutes or until golden brown.

Annie Johnston, China Grove, North Carolina

CRACKLING BREAD

3 c. cornmeal	1 c. milk
1 tsp. salt	1 c. chopped cracklings
3 tsp. baking powder	

Sift the cornmeal, salt and baking powder together into a bowl, then stir in the milk. Stir in cracklings and pour into a heated greased skillet. Bake in 425-degree oven for about 25 minutes or until done.

Mrs. P. A. Henry, Baker, Florida

FRIED CORN DODGERS

1 c. cornmeal	1 tsp. salt
1/2 c. self-rising flour	Boiling water

Sift the cornmeal, flour and salt together into a bowl and stir in enough boiling water to make a stiff dough. Shape into biscuit-shaped cakes. Fry in small amount of fat in a frying pan over low heat until golden brown. 4 servings.

Mrs. Kenneth B. Swain, Jr., Raleigh, North Carolina

CORN STICKS

1 c. cornmeal	1 c. buttermilk
2 tbsp. flour	1 egg
1 tsp. salt	1/4 c. salad oil
1/2 tsp. soda	

Preheat oven to 450 degrees. Sift the cornmeal, flour, salt and soda together into a bowl. Add the buttermilk and egg and mix. Add the oil and mix well. Spoon into heated, greased corn stick pan. Bake for 8 minutes, then broil until golden brown. 12 medium corn sticks.

Mrs. P. T. Tomlin, Gilliam, Louisiana

LOUISIANA HUSH PUPPIES

1 1/2 c. cornmeal	4 green onions, chopped
1/2 c. flour	1 egg
1/8 tsp. salt	1 c. buttermilk
2 tbsp. baking powder	4 tbsp. melted bacon drippings
1/2 tsp. soda	Peanut oil

Mix first 5 ingredients in a bowl. Add remaining ingredients except oil and mix well. Drop by spoonfuls into hot peanut oil in deep fryer and cook until golden brown.

Mrs. Robert C. Lowther, Alexandria, Louisiana

OLD-FASHIONED SOUTHERN SPOON BREAD

1 1/2 c. water	1 c. cornmeal
1 tsp. salt	2 eggs, separated
2 tbsp. butter	1 c. milk

Combine the water, salt and butter in a saucepan and bring to a boil. Remove from heat. Add the cornmeal and mix until smooth. Stir in the beaten egg yolks. Add the milk slowly, stirring constantly, then cool. Beat the egg whites until stiff peaks form and fold into cornmeal mixture. Pour into a greased 1-quart baking dish. Bake at 350 degrees for about 1 hour. 6 servings.

Laura Jane Walls, Lewisburg, West Virginia

PLANTATION CORN BREAD

1 1/2 c. cornmeal	1 tbsp. baking powder
1/2 c. flour	1 egg
1 tsp. salt	1 3/4 c. milk
1/2 tsp. sugar	3 tbsp. cooking oil

Combine the cornmeal, flour, salt, sugar and baking powder in a bowl. Add remaining ingredients except oil and mix well. Pour the oil into an iron skillet and heat. Pour the cornmeal mixture into the skillet. Bake at 400 degrees for 30 to 40 minutes. Place on a plate and cut into wedges.

Ruby Little, Bossier City, Louisiana

APRICOT COFFEE CAKE

1 c. chopped dried apricots	4 eggs
1 c. currants	2 1/2 c. sifted flour
1 c. butter	1 tsp. baking powder
1 1/2 c. sugar	

Soak the apricots and currants in water for 1 hour, then drain. Cream the butter and sugar in a bowl. Add the eggs, one at a time, beating well after each addition. Stir in the apricots and currants. Sift the flour with baking powder and stir into the sugar mixture. Pour into a greased and floured loaf pan. Bake at 350 degrees for 1 hour or until done.

Mrs. Violet S. Seelhorst, Galveston, Texas

COCONUT PRALINE COFFEE CAKE

2/3 c. evaporated milk	2 pkg. dry yeast
3/4 c. sugar	1/2 c. warm water
1/2 tsp. salt	2/3 c. (firmly packed) light
2 eggs	brown sugar
3/4 c. soft butter	2/3 c. flaked coconut
Sifted all-purpose flour	Praline Frosting

Place the evaporated milk, sugar, salt and eggs in large bowl of electric mixer and beat until mixed. Add 1/2 cup butter and 2 cups flour and beat with mixer until smooth. Dissolve the yeast in warm water. Add with 1 cup flour to the milk mixture and beat at medium speed for 3 minutes. Stir in 2 cups flour and cover. Let rise for about 1 hour and 30 minutes or until doubled in bulk. Punch down. Turn out onto a well-floured pastry cloth or board and knead lightly. Roll out into a 10 x 15-inch rectangle. Mix remaining butter, brown sugar, 2 tablespoons flour and coconut and spread on the dough. Roll from long side as for jelly roll and place, seam side down, in a greased 10-inch tube pan. Press ends together to seal, then cover. Let rise for about 1 hour or until doubled in bulk. Bake at 350 degrees for 45 minutes and remove from pan. Frost with Praline Frosting while warm. Decorate with pecan halves, if desired.

Praline Frosting

1/4 c. (firmly packed) brown	2 tbsp. melted butter
sugar	1 c. unsifted confectioners'
2 tbsp. evaporated milk	sugar

Combine the brown sugar, evaporated milk and butter in a bowl. Add the confectioners' sugar and beat until smooth.

Photograph for this recipe on page 174.

Jolly Prune Coffee Ring (below)

JOLLY PRUNE COFFEE RING

12 California pitted prunes	1/2 c. chopped walnuts
12 pineapple wedges	2 c. biscuit mix
1/3 c. melted butter or	1/4 c. sugar
margarine	1 tsp. cinnamon
3 tbsp. brown sugar	

Stuff prunes with pineapple wedges and drain on absorbent paper. Place 3 tablespoons butter in bottom of a 9-inch ring mold and sprinkle with brown sugar and half the walnuts. Arrange stuffed prunes on walnut mixture. Prepare drop biscuit batter according to package directions and drop a heaping tablespoon on top of each prune in mold. Brush top with remaining butter. Combine the sugar and cinnamon, and sprinkle over batter with remaining walnuts. Bake in 400-degree oven for 20 to 25 minutes. 6-8 servings.

APPLE COFFEE CAKE

3 eggs	2 tsp. vanilla
2 c. sugar	3 c. chopped apples
1 c. salad oil	1/2 c. margarine
3 c. flour	1 c. (packed) brown sugar
1/2 tsp. salt	1/2 c. evaporated milk
1 tsp. soda	

Mix the eggs, sugar and oil in a bowl. Sift the flour, salt and soda together and stir into the sugar mixture. Stir in the vanilla and apples. Place in a greased loaf pan. Bake at 350 degrees for 30 minutes. Mix remaining ingredients in a saucepan and cook for 2 minutes and 30 seconds, stirring constantly. Pour over coffee cake.

Mrs. Idell Herring, Newton Grove, North Carolina

DELICIOUS WAFFLES

2 1/4 c. sifted flour	2 eggs, beaten
4 tsp. baking powder	2 1/4 c. milk
3/4 tsp. salt	1/4 c. salad oil
1 1/2 tbsp. sugar	

Sift dry ingredients together into a bowl. Combine the eggs, milk and oil and add to flour mixture. Stir just until flour is moistened. Bake in hot waffle iron until brown. 10-12 waffles.

Mrs. Tom Cleveland, Johnson City, Tennessee

FRENCH CHEESE PUFF

1 c. milk	4 eggs
1/4 c. butter	3/4 c. cubed Gruyere or Swiss
1 tsp. salt	cheese
Dash of pepper	2 tbsp. grated Gruyere or Swiss
1 c. sifted flour	cheese

Pour the milk into a saucepan and add the butter, salt and pepper. Bring to a boil. Add the flour all at once and cook over low heat, stirring constantly, until mixture leaves side of pan and forms ball. Remove from heat and beat in eggs, one at a time. Mix in the cubed cheese and cool. Shape 3/4 of the dough into balls, using 1/4 cup for each, and place on a greased baking sheet in shape of a ring. Shape remaining dough into balls, using 1 teaspoon for each, and place on top of and between balls in ring. Sprinkle with grated cheese. Bake at 375 degrees for 45 minutes. 8 servings.

Mrs. Olean McGuire, Jacksonville, Florida

FRENCH LOST BREAD

3 eggs	1/2 tsp. cinnamon or nutmeg
3 tbsp. sugar	6 slices bread

Beat the eggs in a bowl. Add the sugar and cinnamon and mix well. Dip bread into egg mixture. Fry in hot, deep fat until edges begin to brown. Remove from fat and drain. Serve hot.

Mrs. Helen W. Hornsby, Denham Springs, Louisiana

GRAHAM BREAD

2 c. sour milk	1 c. flour
2/3 c. sugar	1 tsp. soda
2 c. (heaping) graham flour	1/2 tsp. salt

Mix the sour milk and sugar in a bowl. Sift the graham flour, flour, soda and salt together and stir into milk mixture. Place in a greased loaf pan. Bake at 350 degrees for 1 hour.

Mrs. Judy Clayton, Chapel Hill, North Carolina

FRENCH BREAD

1 pkg. dry yeast	1 tbsp. salt
3 tbsp. soft shortening	Cornmeal
6 to 6 1/2 c. sifted	1 egg white, slightly beaten
all-purpose flour	

Pour 2 cups warm water into a mixing bowl and sprinkle with yeast. Stir until dissolved. Add the shortening, 4 cups flour and salt and beat until smooth. Add enough remaining flour gradually to make a stiff dough, mixing well after each addition. Turn out onto a floured board and knead until smooth and elastic. Place in a greased bowl and turn to grease top. Cover. Let rise in a warm place, free from draft for about 1 hour and 30 minutes or until doubled in bulk, then punch down. Let rise for about 30 minutes or until almost doubled in bulk. Punch down and divide in half. Shape into long loaves, tapering ends. Sprinkle greased baking sheet with cornmeal and place loaves on the cornmeal. Make several gashes about 1/4 inch deep in each loaf. Let rise for about 1 hour or until doubled in bulk. Place a shallow pan of boiling water on bottom rack of oven. Mix the egg white with 2 tablespoons water and brush on loaves. Bake in 400-degree oven for 20 minutes. Brush with egg mixture and bake for 20 minutes longer or until brown. Cool.

Mrs. Marjorie Williamson, Waxahachie, Texas

SOURDOUGH BREAD

1 c. Sourdough Starter	2 tsp. sugar
6 c. (about) unsifted flour	2 tsp. salt
1 1/2 c. hot water	1 pkg. dry yeast

Mix the Sourdough Starter, 2 cups flour and hot water in a large bowl. Add the sugar and salt and mix. Dissolve the yeast according to package directions and stir into mixture in the bowl. Add remaining flour and mix well. Turn out on floured board and knead until smooth. Shape into 2 loaves. Place in a lightly greased baking pan and cover. Let rise until doubled in bulk, then brush with water. Make diagonal slashes across top and place baking pan in pan of water. Bake at 400 degrees until crust is medium-dark.

Sourdough Starter

6 potatoes	1 c. lukewarm water
2 qt. boiling water	1/3 c. sugar
1 pkg. yeast	3 tbsp. salt

Cook the potatoes in boiling water until tender. Drain and reserve the water. Dissolve the yeast in lukewarm water. Mash the potatoes in a large bowl and stir in the yeast. Add remaining ingredients and reserved potato water and mix well. Leave in the bowl or place in a crock. Cover and leave in a warm place for about 48 hours to ferment. Place in jars and store in a cold place.

Mrs. Kate Fuller, Tampa, Florida

PERFECT WHITE BREAD

1 pkg. dry yeast	2 tsp. salt
1/4 c. water	2 tbsp. shortening
2 c. milk, scalded	6 to 6 1/4 c. sifted
2 tbsp. sugar	all-purpose flour

Dissolve the yeast in warm water. Combine the milk, sugar, salt and shortening in a bowl and cool to lukewarm. Stir in 2 cups flour. Add the yeast and mix. Add enough remaining flour to make a stiff dough. Turn out on a lightly floured surface and knead until smooth. Shape in a ball and place in a lightly greased bowl, turning once to grease surface. Cover and let rise in warm place until doubled in bulk. Shape into 2 loaves and place in greased 8 1/2 x 4 1/2 x 2 1/2-inch loaf pans. Let rise until doubled in bulk. Bake in 350-degree oven for 45 minutes or until brown.

Mrs. Rolfe Taylor, Elk Creek, Virginia

CREOLE CASSEROLE BREAD

1 c. milk	2 pkg. dry yeast
3 tbsp. dark brown sugar	1 tsp. cinnamon
1 tbsp. salt	1/2 tsp. nutmeg
2 tbsp. margarine	4 c. unsifted flour
1 c. warm water	

Scald the milk and stir in the sugar, salt and margarine. Cool to lukewarm. Pour the water into a large, warm bowl. Sprinkle with yeast, and stir until dissolved. Add the milk mixture, cinnamon, nutmeg and flour and stir for about 2 minutes or until well blended. Cover and let rise in a warm place, free from draft, for about 1 hour or until more than doubled in bulk. Stir down and beat vigorously for about 30 seconds. Turn into a greased 1 1/2 quart casserole. Bake immediately in a 375-degree oven for about 1 hour or until done.

Creole Casserole Bread (above)

COCONUT BREAD

3 c. all-purpose flour
1 tbsp. baking powder
1/2 tsp. salt
1 c. sugar

1 c. shredded coconut
1 egg, beaten
1 c. milk
1 tsp. vanilla

Preheat oven to 350 degrees. Sift first 4 ingredients together into a bowl. Add the coconut and mix thoroughly. Combine remaining ingredients. Stir into dry ingredients and mix well. Let stand for 20 minutes. Pour into a well-greased 9 x 5 x 3-inch loaf pan. Bake for 45 to 50 minutes or until bread tests done.

Rebecca L. Crookshanks, Fredericksburg, Virginia

RICE MUFFINS

1 egg, beaten
1 c. milk
1 c. cooked rice
1 1/2 c. flour
4 tsp. baking powder

1/2 tsp. salt
3 strips cooked crisp bacon,
    crumbled
Tart jelly

Mix the egg, milk and rice in a bowl. Sift the flour with baking powder and salt and stir into egg mixture. Place the bacon in greased muffin cups and pour batter over bacon, filling cups 1/2 full. Bake at 425 degrees for 30 minutes. Top each muffin with a spoon of jelly.

Mrs. Otto Murphy, Springfield, Tennessee

SOPAIPILLA

1 c. sifted flour
1 tsp. baking powder
1/2 tsp. salt

1 tsp. shortening
1/4 c. buttermilk
1/4 c. water

Sift the flour, baking powder and salt together into a bowl and cut in the shortening. Stir in the buttermilk and water until mixed. Roll out on a floured surface about 1/8 inch thick. Fold over and roll out again to 1/8-inch thickness. Cut into 3-inch triangles or squares. Cook in deep, hot fat until golden brown. Sprinkle with powdered sugar or serve with syrup or honey, if desired.

Mrs. Nettie Gray, Columbus, Georgia

CINNAMON BUNS

2/3 c. scalded milk
Sugar
1 1/4 tsp. salt
6 tbsp. shortening
2/3 c. lukewarm water
3 pkg. yeast

3 eggs, beaten
6 c. flour
1 c. (packed) brown sugar
1/2 c. raisins
2 tsp. cinnamon
Powdered sugar glaze

Mix the milk, 1/2 cup sugar, salt and shortening in a bowl and cool to lukewarm. Mix the water, 3 tablespoons sugar and yeast and add to milk mixture. Add the eggs. Stir in 3 cups flour and beat until smooth. Add remaining flour and mix well. Turn out on a floured surface and knead until smooth and elastic. Place in a greased bowl and cover. Let rise in warm place until doubled in bulk. Roll out on a floured surface into rectangular shape and grease. Sprinkle with a mixture of brown sugar, raisins and cinnamon. Roll as for jelly roll and cut into slices. Place on a baking sheet and let rise until doubled in bulk. Bake at 425 degrees for 20 minutes and top with powdered sugar glaze.

Mrs. Faye Dixon, China Grove, North Carolina

HOT CAKES

2 c. flour	2 c. milk
4 tsp. baking powder	2 eggs
1 tsp. salt	1 tsp. melted shortening
2 tsp. sugar	

Sift the flour, baking powder, salt and sugar together 5 times and place in a bowl. Add the milk, eggs and shortening and beat well. Drop by spoonfuls on a hot griddle and cook until bubbles appear. Turn and brown on other side. 4-5 servings.

Mary Ann Plott, Durham, North Carolina

SPANISH ROSQUILLAS

1 c. flour	1/4 tsp. vanilla
1/3 c. sugar	2 tbsp. softened butter
1 egg	Melted butter or margarine
1 tsp. baking powder	Powdered sugar

Place the flour, sugar, egg, baking powder, vanilla and softened butter in a mixing bowl and mix until smooth. Leave in a warm place to rise slightly. Shape into half moons about the diameter of a silver dollar. Fry in a small amount of melted butter in a skillet for about 4 minutes on each side or until brown. Sprinkle with powdered sugar and serve warm. 18 cakes.

Mrs. Phillip Meade, Tucson, Arizona

RICE GRIDDLE CAKES

1 c. sifted flour	1 1/2 c. milk
2 tsp. baking powder	2 eggs, separated
1/2 tsp. salt	1 tbsp. melted shortening
1 1/2 c. cooked rice	

Sift dry ingredients together. Place the rice in a bowl and pour the milk over rice. Add beaten egg yolks and shortening and mix well. Stir in the dry ingredients. Fold in the beaten egg whites. Drop by spoonfuls onto a hot greased griddle and cook until brown on both sides, turning once.

Mrs. Eloise Williams, Greenville, Texas

Whole Wheat Doughnuts (below)

WHOLE WHEAT DOUGHNUTS

3/4 c. milk
3/4 c. (firmly packed) dark
  brown sugar
1/2 tsp. salt
1/4 c. margarine
1/4 c. dark molasses
1/2 c. warm water

2 pkg. dry yeast
2 eggs
3 c. unsifted whole wheat
  flour
2 3/4 c. unsifted (about)
  flour
Peanut oil

Scald the milk and stir in the brown sugar, salt, margarine and molasses. Cool to lukewarm. Pour the water into a large, warm bowl. Sprinkle with yeast and stir until dissolved. Stir in the molasses mixture, eggs and whole wheat flour and beat until well blended. Stir in enough flour to make a soft dough. Turn out onto a lightly floured board and knead for about 10 minutes or until smooth and elastic. Place in a greased bowl, turning to grease top. Cover and let rise in a warm place, free from draft, for about 1 hour and 15 minutes or until doubled in bulk. Punch down and turn out onto a lightly floured board. Roll out about 1/2 inch thick. Cut with a 2 1/2-inch doughnut cutter. Place doughnuts and holes separately on greased baking sheets. Press remaining dough into a ball. Reroll and cut into doughnuts and holes. Place on greased baking sheets as before. Cover and let rise in a warm place, free from draft, for about 1 hour and 15 minutes or until doubled in bulk. Drop doughnuts and holes, raised side down, into deep oil at 375 degress and fry for about 3 minutes, turning once. Sprinkle with confectioners' sugar or additional sugar, if desired.

A touch of seasonings is an essential part of Creole cookery. Most Creole homes had small kitchen gardens — patches where herbs were grown especially for use in the delicious dishes prepared every day. Today, fresh herbs can be grown in home gardens or in small pots.

Also available today are dried herbs and spices. Dried seasonings lose flavor quickly. Store them in a dry, cool place, and test periodically to be certain that the flavor remains. To test, rub a bit of the seasoning between the palms of your hands. If the aroma of the seasoning is not present, then it should be discarded and a new supply bought.

When using dried herbs, remember that they are four times as potent as fresh ones. If a recipe specifies a teaspoon of fresh herbs, use only a quarter teaspoon dried ones.

seasonings

FOR CREOLE COOKERY

SEASONING	USES IN CREOLE COOKERY
Allspice	One of the native North American seasonings, allspice has the combined flavors of nutmeg, cinnamon, and cloves. It is used whole with berries, fish, meat, or in sauces. Powdered allspice is used in cooked fruits, desserts, vegetables, game, and poultry.
Basil	One of the five essential herbs in the Creole combination known as *fines herbes*. Basil is used by itself in tomato-based dishes, turtle soup, potatoes, game, fish sauces, and with mushrooms.
Bay leaf	A popular seasoning often used in combination with marjoram or rosemary and thyme in stews, sauces, and fish dishes.
Bouquet garni	A cheesecloth bag filled with thyme, parsley, marjoram, celery leaves, and tarragon that is usually steeped in the liquid of soups or stews and removed before serving.
Chive	Another of the five *fines herbes* of Creole cookery. Use by itself in salads, soups, dressings, and with game, fish, and poultry.

SEASONING	USES IN CREOLE COOKERY
Garlic	A touch of this bulb-like seasoning is found in almost all Creole cookery. Rub the pot or dish in which a food will be prepared with a cut clove of garlic for a delicious hint of flavor. Use whole garlic in preparing soups, stews, game, fish, or poultry.
Marjoram	Creole cooks use marjoram in company with thyme and bay leaf in almost every food except sweet dishes. Use marjoram alone in dressings for game.
Mushrooms	Mushrooms are an important seasoning in Creole cookery. While they are botanically a fungus and are most often served in American homes as a vegetable, Creole cooks preferred to use them as a seasoning to complement many dishes.
Onion	Traditionally considered a vegetable, onion is used in an unusual way in Creole cookery. It is baked in a medium to hot oven to a dark brown ("charred") and is then placed in the roasting pan with beef, lamb, or pork roasts.
Pepper	Creole cookery uses many types of pepper. *Black pepper* is used in game, poultry, and fish dished as well as in salads, dressings, soups, and stews. *Cayenne pepper* is used when a hotter pepper than either black or white is desired. *Tobasco* is a liquid pepper sauce made from the hot pepper. It is so potent that only a drop or two is required to season a dish.
Savory	Another of the Creole *fines herbes*, savory is used alone in egg dishes, dressings, dried beans, squash, eggplant, stews, and stuffings.
Tarragon	Another of the Creole *fines herbes*, tarragon is prized for its slightly licorice flavor. It is used in pickles, salad dressings, sauces, and in almost all seafood dishes.
Truffles	Truffles, a fungus growth, are an important part of Creole cookery. They are found only in France and are imported. Both truffles and mushrooms are considered essential ingredients in sauces, soups, main dishes, and meat, poultry, and fish cookery.

INDEX

PHOTOGRAPHY CREDITS: National Fisheries Institute; California Avocado Advisory Board; Knox Gelatine; Apple Pantry: Washington State Apple Commission; South African Rock Lobster Service Corporation; American Mushroom Institute; Best Foods, a Division of CPC International Inc.; Rice Council; Processed Apples Institute; General Foods Kitchens; Cling Peach Advisory Board; American Lamb Council; Keith Thomas Company; National Dairy Council; U. S. Department of Commerce: National Marine Fisheries Service; The American Spice Trade Association; Frozen Potato Products Institute; Evaporated Milk Association; California Prune Advisory Board; Olive Administrative Committee; Standard Brands Products: Fleischmann's Yeast, Fleischmann's Margarine; National Macaroni Institute; Brussels Sprouts Marketing Program; Spanish Green Olive Commission; Louisiana Yam Commission; Pickle Packers International; Sunkist Growers; Canned Salmon Institute; McIlhenny Company; United Fresh Fruit and Vegetable Association; The Nestle Company; Ocean Spray Cranberries, Inc.

Printed in the United States of America.